Homelessness and Drinking: A Study of a Street Population

Homelessness and Drinking: A Study of a Street Population

114 4323

Bernard Segal, PhD

362.29
Se 37

The Haworth Press, Inc.
New York • London • Sydney

Homelessness and Drinking: A Study of a Street Population has also been published as *Drugs & Society*, Volume 5, Numbers 3/4 1991.

The Haworth Press, Inc., 10 Alice Street, Binghamton, NY 13904-1580
EUROSPAN/Haworth, 3 Henrietta Street, London WC2E 8LU England
ASTAM/Haworth, 162-168 Parramatta Road, Stanmore, Sydney, N.S.W. 2048 Australia

Library of Congress Cataloging-in-Publication Data

Segal, Bernard.
    Homelessness and drinking : a study of a street population / Bernard Segal.
      p. cm.
    "Also ... published as Drugs & Society, volume 5, numbers 3/4, 1991."
    Includes bibliographical references.
    ISBN 1-56024-210-8 (acid free paper)
    1. Homeless persons — Alaska — Anchorage — Alcohol use — Case studies. 2. Skid row — Alaska — Anchorage — Case studies. I. Title.
HV5140.S44 1991
362.29'22'086942 — dc20
                                              91-25836
                                              CIP

Homelessness and Drinking:
A Study of a Street Population

CONTENTS

ABOUT THE AUTHOR

Bernard Segal, PhD, is Professor of Health Sciences at the University of Alaska in Anchorage. He has a lengthy association with the University in Anchorage, having held numerous positions there since 1977. Dr. Segal's research interest is in the etiology, epidemiology, and psychosocial correlates of drug-taking behavior, with special emphasis on Alaskan issues. A recipient of both federal and state research grants, his research has led to two books, numerous publications and presentations, and to collaboration with researchers in other countries, such as Israel, Japan, and the USSR. Dr. Segal's more recent research has featured a comprehensive follow-up study of drug-taking behavior among Alaskan youth in grades 7-12. His work has become the "benchmark" in Alaska for assessing the extent and pattern of drug use among youth during the past decade.

Foreword

A Skid Row has been described as a place where homeless people, primarily men, congregate after having "dropped out" from "normal" societal functions or demands, and who group together in order to drink and to sustain themselves. Anchorage has an active Skid Row population characterized by homelessness and a high level of drinking behavior. This report characterizes the homeless population, and provides a description of their drinking behavior. The estimated level of problem-related drinking among the homeless greatly exceeded prevalence levels for the general population estimated at 11 to 15 percent for men and 2 to 4 percent for women. The findings also exceeded the rate of alcoholism reported in other studies, which estimated that approximately 25 to 40 percent of homeless men suffer from serious alcohol problems. The level of drinking among the Anchorage Skid Row population also exceeded the findings from four major Skid Row surveys that found that between 33 to 40 percent of the Skid Row residents drank to excess. The general characteristics of the street population was one of mostly men (8 out of every 10 persons), largely between 26 and 35 years of age, of which two out of ten are White, seven out of ten Alaska Native, and one out of ten being either Black, Hispanic, Asian or from other ethnic groups. Over half (50.7%) have never married. A majority have completed a high school education. About one in three served in a branch of the armed forces, with just over one in ten having been to Vietnam. A discussion of the implications of the findings is presented, and issues concerning intervention are discussed.

Preface

This report conveys a multitude of information about a homeless drinking population in Anchorage, Alaska. The data presented were obtained from ongoing day-to-day observations of individuals using a Sleep-Off Center. These observations also included estimates of blood alcohol levels (BAL) obtained by a breathalyzer administered on entry to the shelter, and from an in-depth interview with a large sample of the daily shelter users. The data that was compiled provided a unique opportunity to monitor the drinking behavior of a street population, and to study this behavior in relation to demographic, sociological, and other pertinent variables. This monograph thus presents a comprehensive analysis of the data, often analyzing similar data, such as drinking levels represented through BAL measurements, from different perspectives.

Although the data presented in this study are extensive, and the focus is limited to a specific population in Anchorage, Alaska, the nature of the findings and its implications are important. The classic Skid Rows of the 1930s are essentially gone, replaced by street populations chiefly comprised of members of different ethnic groups, largely members of minority populations. These newer groups present a unique challenge to health and governmental authorities struggling to deal with them. The findings from this study have implications for responding to the needs of these populations. For example, from a general perspective, it was surmised that the situation in Anchorage illustrates how social agencies are exploited by clients to perpetuate their unhealthy lifestyle, leading to the conclusion that a strategy needs to be developed to break the Skid Row lifestyle and to coordinate how different agencies respond to clients manipulating the system. A scheme has been proposed to develop a coordinated approach. From a more specific perspective, it has also been shown how any effort to alter a street lifestyle cannot be achieved unless cultural aspects are made part of the intervention process. For example, Native Americans cannot be expected to make a transition from a self-destructive, nevertheless peer-supported, street lifestyle to a healthier alcohol-free life without first confronting their feeling concerning loss of their cultural identity.

Therefore the Alaskan focus not only provides a look at a special population in a unique environment, but the findings also have significant implications to similar populations in other locations. It is the expectation that the findings and perspectives provided will contribute to a better understanding of the needs of a contemporary, ethnically dominate, homeless, drinking population.

Bernard Segal, PhD

Acknowledgments

The preparation of this report involved many people, and their contribution is appreciated. But none was more crucial than the assistance given by Sue Ann Pennington, my research assistant. She was responsible for the supervision of data collection and for the development of the data base. Without Sue the study would never have occurred.

Dr. Raymond Dexter, Executive Director of the Clitheroe Alcoholism Treatment program, Anchorage, Alaska, who was successful in winning the research and demonstration grant that funded this project, was invaluable in facilitating what needed to be done. Joan Booth, Director of the Sleep-Off Center and her staff, as well as members of the Clitheroe program, also provided valuable assistance. Margaret Lambert, my departmental secretary, was, as usual, extremely helpful. Her assistance is gratefully recognized.

The assistance provided by the staff of the Computer & Technology Services program, University of Alaska Anchorage, is deeply appreciated. Its Director, Ron Langley, always cheerful and supportive, creates an atmosphere where research is a pleasure. I am especially gratefully for the generous assistance given by Victor J. Kapella, Systems Manager, who helped work out statistical programs, solved problems, and who did an untold number of big and little things which added up to a substantial contribution to the task of data analysis.

My friend, Matthew Schall, who no longer lives the life of an ABD, gave valuable consultation on statistical methods.

Don Cahalan, Ph.D., who I somehow never quite let fully enjoy the fruits of retirement, reviewed the manuscript and provided helpful comments.

To all those mentioned, and to others who were supportive of this project, who are not directly identified, I express my thanks and appreciation.

Lastly, to the unsung heroine, my wife Marjorie, thanks for all your help.

Chapter 1

Introduction

This report conveys findings from a study of a homeless population in Anchorage, Alaska. The data was derived from a comprehensive research and demonstration project[1] designed to intervene in the lifestyle of homeless drinkers. The project, entitled "Treating Homeless and Dual Diagnosis Substance Abusers," was conducted by the Salvation Army's Clitheroe Alcoholism Treatment Program, Anchorage, Alaska.

The project called for a coordinated approach revolving around the establishment of a 24-hour sobering center ("Sleep-Off Center") in which homeless street people, many of whom would be intoxicated, could find shelter. It was planned for the SOC to serve as a hub in which mental health outreach workers, alcohol counselors, and other human service providers would be available to initiate active case-finding. The basic notion was that when homeless public inebriates were sheltered in a safe place there would be an opportunity to motivate them into treatment. The professionally trained staff would offer "on the spot" initial screening evaluations and make appropriate referrals. Special emphasis would be given to identifying mentally ill drug abusers (i.e., dually diagnosed individuals), so that appropriate referrals and interventions could be made that addressed their specialized needs. In essence, the SOC was to serve as a specialized "catchment center" to attempt to bring people into treatment.

This report is based on data derived from this project, which started on January 6, 1988, when the shelter officially opened. The research was not perceived as an investigation into the nature and causes of alcoholism or drug abuse, or for developing analytical predictors of successful outcomes, but some information obtained

1

could be used to help shed light on these problems. The research concentrated on identifying the population using the shelter, and on assessing the impact of an intervention process.

An important element of the research involved development of a research design (i.e., methodology and assessment techniques) that was culturally relevant and sensitive to not one, but several distinct racial/ethnic minorities. The development of the instrumentation presented difficulties beyond the problems ordinarily encountered in more traditional research. Such difficulties surface not only when attempting to use available data that may or may not be recognized as biased, but also in designing new measures, and in striving for interpretations that accurately reflect reality as it is perceived and experienced by different racial/ethnic groups, or subpopulations (e.g., street people), themselves. Thus the measures that were developed had to be responsive to these issues.

The project created an opportunity for an in-depth, comprehensive study of the characteristics and behaviors of homeless chronic drinkers, who constitute what has been identified as Anchorage's Skid Row (Kelso, Hobfoll, & Peterson, 1978). When this information is linked to treatment outcome data, then current, valid information about behaviors of clients at the inception of, during, and after treatment, is obtainable. Researchers, federal, state, and local governmental agencies, individual programs, and the general public are in need of such information to further an understanding about intervention/treatment effectiveness for special clinical populations. Moreover, fundamental information about the nature of the homeless (or Skid Row) population would also be vital in attempting to help understand more about the needs of this population, as well as provide a data base to help evaluate any attempt to reduce the adverse impacts of drinking among members of a Skid Row population.

A BRIEF REVIEW OF HOMELESSNESS

The problem of homelessness in American society has been a long-standing one, but it has not been until recently that an in-depth attempt was made to begin to understand the nature and scope of the problem (Institute, 1988). Not only have uniform definitions of "homeless" been lacking, but attempts to estimate the number of homeless left uncertainty about their numbers. The problem was also complicated because the homeless have traditionally been characterized as an alcoholic and impoverished group who represent a "Skid Row" subpopulation (Blumberg, Shipley, & Barsky, 1978).

A Skid Row has been described as a place where homeless people, primarily men, congregate after having "dropped out" from "normal" societal functions or demands, and who group together to drink and to sustain themselves. The image of a Skid Row can be traced back to the concept of post-Civil War hoboemia described by Anderson (1923). By the beginning of the 20th Century many cities began to experience the emergence of run-down neighborhoods, called "Skid Rows," whose inhabitants consisted of largely unskilled older male laborers (over 50 years) rendered homeless due to economic influences (McCook, 1893). Many of these inhabitants had been arrested at least once for drunkenness.

The image of the Skid Row that emerged during the early 1900s was that of an impaired population characterized by excessive drinking, mental illness, criminal behavior and senility, which prevented them from working (Solenberger, 1911). This characterization contrasted with the finding of Cook (1910) who, a year earlier, described the men he interviewed as recently employed and of good character but as having turned to criminality by becoming homeless and being mistreated.

Skid Rows, however, did not become a major concern in America until the depression era, during which a marked increase in the homeless population was noted nationwide. Although studies of these populations in different locations reported deviations in the prevalence of various demographic characteristics, there was a generally consistent report of drinking, physical illness, including disabilities and mental illness (Stark, 1987).

The country's involvement in World War II resulted in a pause in efforts to deal with the homeless, and interest in this group receded until the late 1940s. Straus (1946), in a comprehensive study of the homeless, indicated that the relationship between homelessness and alcoholism "is striking." Homelessness, however, as described by Straus, is a complex condition encompassing a constellation of behavioral patterns, attitudes and social situations. He also described alcoholism as a complex condition and speculated about what alcoholism and homelessness had in common. Strauss found that such elements as parental influence, occupational status, and sociocultural factors were all related to these two conditions. Subsequent research by Straus and McCarthy (1951) found that although pathological drinking was present among most homeless men, a substantial portion of those men were not alcoholics.

The 1950s saw a shift to interest in "inner-city" problems, one of which involved a re-examination of Skid Row populations. Historically, the Skid Row population was equated with congregated street scenes, but it had apparently changed from the stereotype of the vagrant to more isolated islands of single room occupancy dispersed in different neighborhoods in cities (Siegal, Peterson & Chambers, 1975). These changes were attributed to urban renewal, expanded social security coverage, and increased difficulty in finding jobs due to advances in technology.

The research of the 1950s and 1960s reported that alcohol was present in varying proportions of homeless men living in Skid Row districts in different inner cities. Estimates ranged from 16.6 percent in Chicago in 1958, to 26 to 36 percent in New York City during 1963 and 1968, to 38 percent in Minneapolis in the early 1980s (Stark, 1987). Other common features found among Skid Row populations were mental illness, severe physical handicaps and unemployment. The Skid Row population generally tended to consist of older, primarily white homeless men who had developed their own subculture (Blumberg, Shipley, & Moor, 1971).

This Skid Row configuration started to change during the 1970s. It was becoming younger, encompassed more members of minority groups, and began to include Vietnam veterans. An increase in the number of mentally ill homeless and drug users was also noted (Reich & Siegel, 1978). Changes in the traditional Skid Row population were observed well into the 1980s. Homelessness groups now started to include increasing numbers of the elderly, women, children, minorities, the unemployed, displaced families, and the mentally ill (NIAAA, 1987).

The Skid Row emerged as a special gathering place for minority members of American society, especially for Native Americans. The emergence of the Skid Row Native American was seen as the product of a clash between traditional Native American cultures and nonnative or White value systems, resulting in significant acculturation stress (Heath, 1989). Graves (1971) suggested that the drunkenness, unemployment, police involvement, etc., are not inherently features of Indian behavior, but represent the impact of surrounding social structures that are similar for all people who are members of the same disadvantaged, economically deprived class. Westermeyer (1987) indicated that when attempting to comprehend drinking and drug use among members of minority groups, it is essential to consider that different societies ascribe different meaning, values, and attitudes to such behavior, and that an array of psychological, social and cultural interactions are related to different patterns of alcohol and drug use.

HOMELESSNESS IN ANCHORAGE

Anchorage is a relatively isolated community, lying between rugged snow-covered mountains, and Cook Inlet. One only needs to travel a few miles outside the city limits to discover pristine wilderness and wildlife. There are but two roads, one North, and one South. Going North, the Glen Highway connects to the Parks Highway, passing Denali National Park and on to Fairbanks. Going Northeast, the Glen highway links into alternative routes through Canada and the connecting 48 states (called the "Lower-48"). Going south of Anchorage the Seward Highway leads to either Homer or Seward. Many communities, especially Alaskan Native communities, are not connected to Anchorage by road. Air transportation is necessary, and this is expensive. Thus geographical isolation and transportation costs make it very difficult for any homeless individual to relocate or to return home after having migrated to Anchorage.

Anchorage has social services not available in other Alaskan communities. Some individuals associated with street life pursue seasonal work through the fishing industry and tend to return to Anchorage for these services.

Anchorage, being in the Southcentral part of the state, usually has a more moderate climate than regions to the north. The weather, however, is variable and unpredictable, with deep cold spells followed by thaws in mid-winter. Annual snow fall averages 70 inches. The coldest month is January when the average high temperature is 22°F. The homeless are particularly vulnerable during the months of December through March when daylight hours and temperatures are at their minimum. Lives are lost every winter despite availability of services. In summer, temperatures average 58 degrees with many days being in the 60 to 70°F range, with 18-19 hours of daylight.

A Skid Row population exists in the downtown district of Anchorage, Alaska. A study of this population (Kelso, Hobfoll, & Peterson, 1980) found that the composite character of the street population was not essentially different from Skid Row populations described in the literature, but that it was exceptional with respect to the high level of alcohol consumed. The largest component of Kelso et al.'s street sample of 206 persons was Alaskan Natives (57.3%), followed by Whites (39.5%), Blacks (2.6%) and Asians (0.5%). Eighty-one percent were men; 19 percent were women. Kelso et al. (1980) concluded that the street population could be classified into four distinguishable subgroups: (1) Homeless-Unemployed, who fit the traditional stereotype of the "public inebriate" that inhabit Skid Row; (2) Highly-Mobile-Working, represented by seasonal workers who migrate to and from Anchorage; (3) Residential-Employed, long-term inhabitants of Anchorage who maintained a residence in the Skid Row area but were able to provide for themselves; and (4) Residential-Semi-Employed, those not clearly defined as members of the other three groups but who went through cycles of employment and unemployment.

The public inebriate, as well as other homeless persons who are not public inebriates, have a significant impact on the neighborhoods and businesses within the downtown area. The study by Kelso et al. (1980) estimated that the total Skid Row population was approximately 700 persons with the chronic public inebriate subgroup being about 90 persons. It is currently estimated that the Skid Row population has at least doubled since 1980.

A 1981 documentary film entitled "4th Avenue," characterized the function of 4th Avenue as a traditional meeting place for people coming into Anchorage from other areas of the State. It is unlikely that would change substantially even if all the facilities for the homeless were removed from the area.

The gathering locations of the Anchorage homeless have frequently changed to avoid harassment. However, they remain within the radius of the downtown area. The flow of movement from the SOC into the downtown core (approximately 1 mile) is a well established pattern. SOC clients hit the streets between 7:30 a.m. and 9:30 a.m. On their way to the downtown core area they usually make a stop at Bean's Cafe for coffee and sweet-rolls. Through panhandling they usually acquire enough money to "pool" their resources to buy a bottle of vodka. Many Alaskan Natives are not financially destitute. They receive monthly dividend checks from their Native corporations, and annual state dividend checks. Nonnative residents also receive their state dividend check. Many street people receive unemployment or welfare checks. Much of this money serves to supply alcohol.

Vodka and whiskey, which have high alcohol content, are preferred. The drinkers gather in groups of two or three outside the liquor store on 13th Avenue and Gambell until they get a bottle. According to the Community Service Patrol (CSP)[2] logs, approximately half the public inebriates picked up by the patrol gather around the liquor store on 13th and Gambell. They then move to a more secluded location, sometimes not, to share stories and the bottle of liquor. Drinking in public has not been an offense since the Uniform Alcohol Act was adopted by the State in the 1970s. Sometimes they gather in the small park area located in front of the old City Hall on 4th Avenue and E Street. According to the CSP logs many CSP pick-ups occur at this park.

The pattern of drinking and telling stories continues through the day and into the early evening hours. During the evening they tend to cluster together on 4th Ave., mostly between C and D streets, frequenting the two remaining bars on the block. They roam the Avenue, some going to the bar a few blocks east. Many are picked up off the street by the CSP van and transported to the SOC. The highly intoxicated, combative public inebriate may be transported by the police to the jail for noncriminal, 12-hour custody when they come to the attention of officers who patrol 4th Avenue and its environs. The less combative are usually talked into a ride to the

SOC by the police. Alaskan Natives who are highly intoxicated or who appear to be ill are transported by the police to the Alaskan Native (Public Health) Medical Center's emergency room where they are retained or treated and released and retransported by the police to the jail or SOC. Those left on the street eventually work their way to the SOC where they can sleep without harassment. Many of these people are homeless and without any family support, resulting in a stable population of individuals "on the Avenue." (The "Avenue" stands for 4th Avenue, the downtown street where "street people" congregate.)

The following chapters characterize these individuals, describe their drinking and other drug-taking behavior, and report on attempts at intervention. It is, in essence, a very comprehensive examination of the homeless public inebriates who constitute Anchorage's Skid Row.

NOTES

1. "Treating Homeless and Dual Diagnosis Substance Abusers," funded by NIAAA Grant No. R18- AA07961.
2. The function of the Community Service Patrol is described in Chapter 3.

Chapter 2

Method

RESEARCH DESIGN

The data used in this study, as noted in Chapter 1, was obtained from an evaluation study that attempted to assess the outcome of treatment intervention that originated at the Sleep-Off Center (SOC). The monitoring of events provided a unique opportunity to characterize a homeless, drinking population, and to describe their treatment involvement.

Given the extensive amount of information obtained, the present research evolved into a detailed descriptive analysis of the homeless population. The population studied consisted of those individuals who entered the Sleep-Off Center between January 6th and December 31, 1989.

Figure 1 conveys a description of the general framework of the original research and demonstration project from which the data for the study were derived. The research scheme, conceived as a "pseudo-continuum" involving different stages or phases, yielded different levels of information at each stage.

Regarding the research scheme, there are different sources from which individuals could enter the Sleep-Off Center, but once an individual entered the SOC, he/she was included in the data base and became part of the study. Additional information was gathered after an individual chose to enter treatment or become involved in some form of intervention. In this context a subsample consisted of individuals who entered treatment.

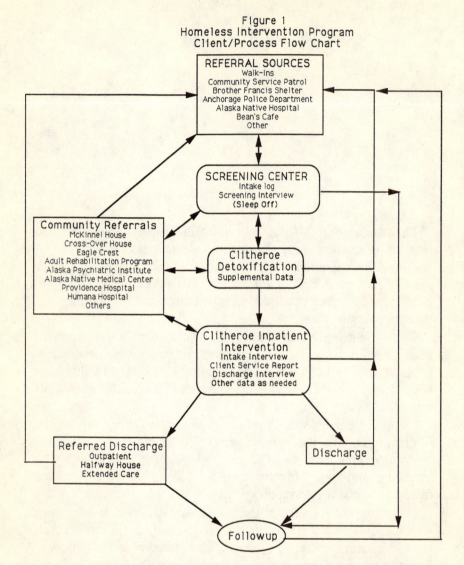

Figure 1
Homeless Intervention Program
Client/Process Flow Chart

INSTRUMENTS AND INSTRUMENT DEVELOPMENT

The current research provides data on the homeless public inebriate. Although its method is in keeping with established procedures some elements of the research are unique. The procedure called for the development of instruments to obtain a wide array of information including demographic data, drinking and drug-taking behavior, social functioning, economic and occupational information and legal involvement. The unique part of the research was that the information had to be obtained in a way that was responsive to people of diverse ethnic backgrounds. An approach was formed that appeared to be sensitive to the needs of Alaskan Natives and other ethnic groups.

Instrument development, with the above consideration in mind, was a major component of the research. It was thought that if the usefulness of the findings were to be maximized all study components had to be carefully integrated. Thus in developing the measures particular attention was given to the comparability of the items used at the different levels of data collection. Misinterpretation of different questions by respondents could lead to serious bias when comparing data from different stages. The different assessment tools were designed to provide consistent data encompassing a broad range of information including, but not limited to, etiological and socioeconomic perspectives. The following is a specific description of the measurements used at each phase of the study, with a rationale for the way in which the instruments were developed.

1. Sleep-Off Center Intake Log

The Sleep-Off Center (SOC), represented in the second oval box shown in Figure 1, was designed to temporarily shelter the homeless and to be the first stage in an intervention process. Coming from a variety of sources, clients using the SOC were targeted for active case finding to recruit them into treatment. All clients were logged in at the time of entry (see Appendix 1, Intake Log). The Intake Log served to identify who used the SOC and to specify client characteristics. Such information as name, residential status, ethnicity, age, gender, entry time, date, blood alcohol level (BAL) on entry, referral source, condition on entry, and use of alcohol and other drugs, were recorded on entry. Upon departure the date and time of leaving, an exit BAL, and destination were recorded.

The Intake Log was maintained by staff members at the SOC, who tried to obtain an entry BAL on all walk-ins. This was a difficult task, initially, because of high intoxication levels, combativeness by some individuals, and resistance by others to give any information. Client resistance was reduced, except for very highly intoxicated and assaultive individuals, by making it mandatory to "blow" (obtain a BAL) and to give the essential information to enter. Many of those creating a disturbance were transported to a hospital or jail by the police. Client resistance was also overcome soon after the SOC staff came to know their names and could relate to them more personally.

The blood alcohol level, obtained by a breathalyzer (an Intoximeter IT 3000 mode), requires that a short breath be blown into a tube to obtain a reading. The IT 3000 is a computerized machine, recalibrated quarterly by a BAL-certified Anchorage Police Officer.

2. Initial Screening Interview (ISI)

Besides monitoring client utilization and assessing client condition through the Intake Log, an Initial Screening Interview (ISI) (see Appendix 2), was used to obtain more detailed information from each client. An attempt was made to obtain a completed form for each client who entered the SOC. This measure was designed to obtain information covering eight areas: (1) demographics, (2) living arrangements, (3) drinking behavior, (4) treatment history, (5) family history, (6) other drug use, (7) legal involvement, and (8) interviewer's assessment.

The design of this instrument, specifically worded and structured to be applicable to multicultural groups, attempted to account for the different educational levels of the clients. It was successfully pilot tested for two months (November and December, 1988). The pilot testing yielded the following information: (a) The variability within the population to be surveyed; (b) The rate of non-response to be expected; (c) The suitability of the method of collecting the data; (d) The adequacy of the questionnaires; (e) The efficiency of the instructions and effectiveness of interviewers; and (f) The adequacy of the codes chosen to represent the questions. The final form of the interview represented the revisions that were made based on the information gained during its pilot testing.

The interview, considered to be specific to the street population, used local terminology and local reference points. Open-ended questions were specifically used for this population to (a) probe for answers, (b) keep it as unstructured as possible, and (c) obtain information that could be coded as continuous data to facilitate more detailed analyses than permitted when categorical data is used. It was also necessary to consider the problems involved when using self-reported data, particularly from a street population. The issue of the reliability and validity of self-reports has been an ongoing one in the field of alcohol research, especially when working with people who are actively drinking. Although recent reports suggest that self-report data is reliable and valid (Sanchez-Craig & Wilkinson, 1987), the data obtained from any clinical population is nevertheless open to questioning. Any attempt to compensate for possible invalid self-reports was made by building redundancy into the measures used. That is, series of similar questions were asked within and across instruments to attempt to check on the consistency of responses, thereby substantiating the accuracy of responses. The information obtained from the ISI was used to establish a data base for street people.

The ISI was also administered by the SOC staff, who were trained in its administration. Because many clients were too inebriated to respond to questions on entry, the scale was given after they "slept off" their drunkenness, usually just before they decided to leave. Not all clients were cooperative and many could not sustain themselves for the time needed to complete it. In many instances sections of the scale were administered over several days to complete it. Once the staff was able to become better acquainted with clients the number of completed ISIs increased.

3. Client Flow

Once a client entered the SOC several options were available. A client could return to the street, choose to enter the detoxification program, or be referred to one of the service agencies listed in the community referral box shown in Figure 1. After detox or a referral to a hospital, clients could be admitted to treatment in Clitheroe's residential program. All referral information was recorded.

In summary, a stepwise longitudinal approach served as a framework for a comprehensive study from which the current data were extracted. The research, based on this model, is limited to an evaluation of the population that used the Sleep-Off Center. Table 1 summarizes the different assessment levels and the major content area associated with each level.

Primary data represents baseline information, with Level II providing comprehensive background details on entries to the SOC. The Secondary Level data pertains to interventions.

Table 1
Data Collection Sources and Content

Primary Level	Data	Measurement Content
I	Intake Log: Maintained at Sleep-off Center by trained staff.	First level intake data used to form a data base for clients entering the project. Lists basic demographic and BACs on entry and leaving SOC.
II	Interview Screening Inventory: Obtained by trained staff at the SOC.	Provides demographic data drinking behavior assessment, drug-taking behavior assessment, education/occupational history, residence information to determine homeless status, previous treatment experience and legal involvement. Used to a more extended data base on individuals with the program.
Secondary Level		
III	Detox Admission: Obtained from treatment program's records by project staff.	Number of times and length of stay in detox program during 1989.
IV	Clitheroe Admissions to treatment programs: Obtained from program's records by project staff.	Number of times admitted, length of stay, and discharge status in 1989.

Chapter 3

Results and Discussion:
Part A.
A Descriptive Analysis of Clients
Using the Sleep-Off Center

PART I. DUPLICATED ADMISSIONS: 1989

From 6 January to 31 December, 1989, a total of 22,282 people used the Sleep-Off Center (SOC) one or more times. This figure is more than double the expectation for the year. Use of the SOC ranged from once to over a hundred times per person during the year. The following is a detailed analysis of the pattern of use and a detailed description of the people who used the SOC. The data are presented in different ways to provide a comprehensive analysis of SOC users.

A. Utilization

(1) Patterns of Use

Figure 2 shows the pattern of monthly entries to the SOC by the 22,282 cases for 1989. There was a very steep increase between January and February and a high number of entries in March, followed by a sharp decrease in March. A bottoming out occurred in June, followed by steady increases. A significant part of this use pattern is attributable to (a) the time the SOC started, (b) seasonal variation, and (c) policy changes.

With respect to the time the SOC started, it was initially slow in

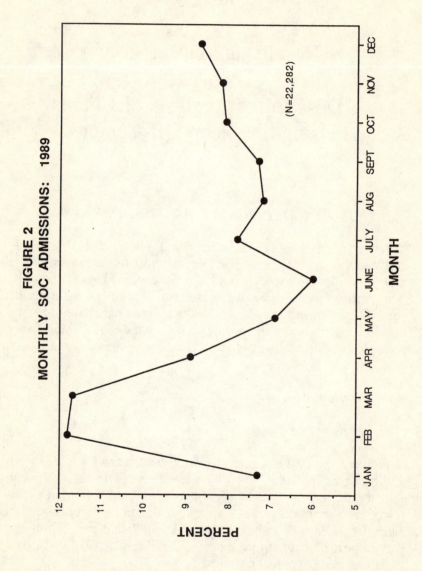

FIGURE 2
MONTHLY SOC ADMISSIONS: 1989

(N=22,282)

PERCENT

MONTH

receiving clients because word had not yet spread about it, and because of a reluctance to use it when its purpose was unclear to the audience it was to serve. Once the SOC was identified as a shelter and it was perceived as not attempting to interfere with client behavior, its use soared.

Seasonal variation also was a factor in the pattern of SOC use. January through March are extremely cold in Anchorage, and during this time the shelter was used by non-intoxicated but homeless persons, many of whom stayed for only one night after arriving in Anchorage, or used it as a place to stay out of the cold for a night or two. The decline started after it began to warm up and people started to seek seasonal employment, such as fishing and working in other seasonal activities. As the weather got colder in the fall people returned to Anchorage and the use rate increased.

Policy changes concerning admission to the SOC were revised after the initial flood of entries in February and March. Because of limited bed space (30 beds) people not intoxicated but seeking shelter were not admitted and sent elsewhere. Priority was given to intoxicated individuals who were judged by the staff not to be in danger of aspirating or possibly going into withdrawal. Additionally, a policy was established to limit the age of entry to 18 years to avoid having the SOC become a youth shelter. These procedural policies had the effect of immediately stabilizing the number of people using the SOC, largely restricting it to public inebriates. The open policy procedure during January to March contributed to the high number of admissions following SOC's opening.

Figure 3 shows a comparison of monthly admissions to the SOC for 1989 and 1990. There was a 31.1 percent increase in 1990 ($N = 29,214$) over 1989 ($N = 22,282$) admissions. Increases in the 1990 admissions started to exceed those in 1989 beginning in March, and continued throughout the remainder of the year.

The use pattern for 1990 generally followed that for 1989, suggesting that the SOC was used more often by both permanent and transient individuals. It is also likely that the SOC was perceived as a stable place to find shelter, resulting in the increase in its use during 1990.

FIGURE 3
MONTHLY SOC ADMISSIONS: 1989 AND 1990

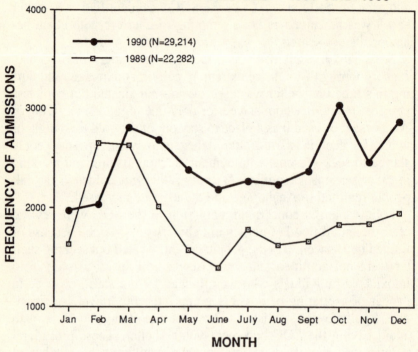

(2) Entries per Person

The total number of entries *per person*, grouped into intervals of ten, appears in Figure 4. Of the 1,749 individuals who entered the SOC in 1989, 75.3 percent entered 10 or fewer times. In contrast, a total of 2.5 percent used the shelter 101 or more times. Cumulatively, 18 percent of the people using the SOC did so between 11 and 50 times. The remaining 4.4 percent entered between 51 and 100 times. While a few cases might be characterized as frequent admissions, most cases entered only once. The SOC appears to have served as a transient center for many of its users, and as a more permanent shelter for homeless street people.

The number of admissions per person for those entering over 101 times is shown in Figure 5. Here, too, as the number of entries in-

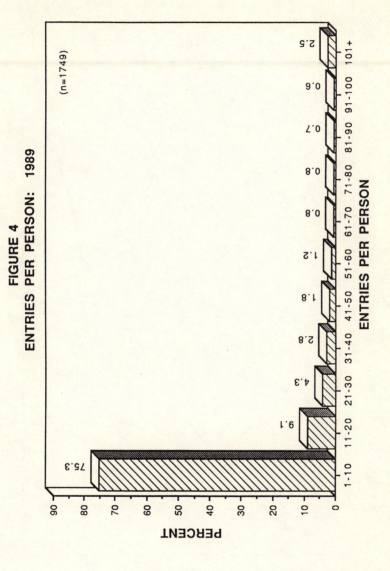

FIGURE 4
ENTRIES PER PERSON: 1989

(n=1749)

Entries Per Person	Percent
1-10	75.3
11-20	9.1
21-30	4.3
31-40	2.8
41-50	1.8
51-60	1.2
61-70	0.8
71-80	0.8
81-90	0.7
91-100	0.6
101+	2.5

19

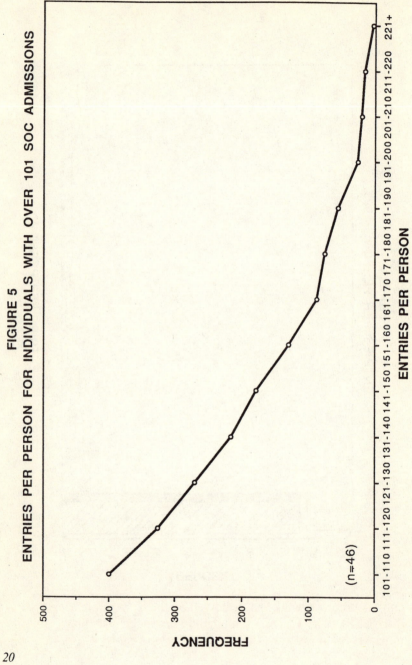

FIGURE 5

ENTRIES PER PERSON FOR INDIVIDUALS WITH OVER 101 SOC ADMISSIONS

(n=46)

FREQUENCY

ENTRIES PER PERSON

20

crease the number of individuals within each entry group decreases. The data is consistent with the previous finding (see Table 4) suggesting that fewer people used the SOC repeatedly.

Figure 6 illustrates the *number* of entries *per person per month* and the *average number of entries per month* for 1989. Inspection of these data show that the 1-10 times entry category predominated, followed by 11-20 times, which was considerably lower. Entries for twenty-one or more times represented only a small proportion of those using the SOC. The average number of admissions per month paralleled the pattern for the number of admissions per month over the year (see Figure 2), but its positioning relative to the frequency of 1-10 admissions per month shows that those who used the SOC ten times or less accounted for the largest percentage of its use.

In summary of SOC use, the early high number of entries settled into a pattern of mostly transient use or people primarily seeking shelter for a night's sleep. After policy changes and familiarity with it by the street people, it quickly emerged as a shelter for the public inebriate, who amounted to fewer than 7 percent of the population using the SOC. The pattern of use of the more transient population was affected by such factors as seasonal variation and alteration in admission policies. Restricting admission largely to those in need — the intoxicated public inebriate — had apparently resulted in a relatively small but steady group of SOC users, supplemented by a more transient group who were nevertheless intoxicated at the time of their admissions after April, 1989. During 1990 the shelter was used more frequently than in 1989, suggesting that not only did a consistent level of street people use the shelter, but also that its use may have increased among intoxicated transients.

B. Admission Data

(1) Entry Sources

Figure 7 depicts the major sources of client entry by month to the SOC during 1989. Observation of these data reveal that the largest entry source was walk-ins, followed by the Community Service Patrol (CSP). The CSP is a medically-equipped van that primarily traverses the downtown district, picking up visibly intoxicated peo-

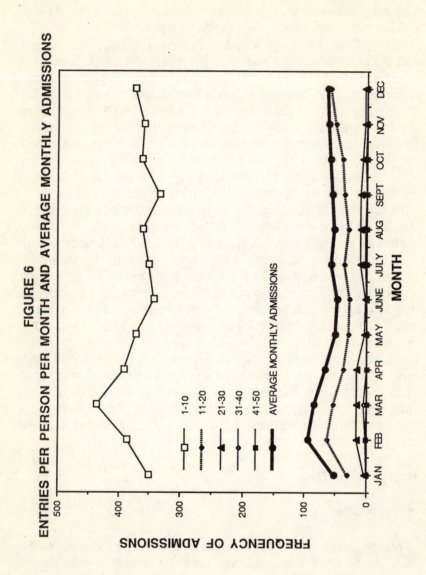

FIGURE 6

ENTRIES PER PERSON PER MONTH AND AVERAGE MONTHLY ADMISSIONS

22

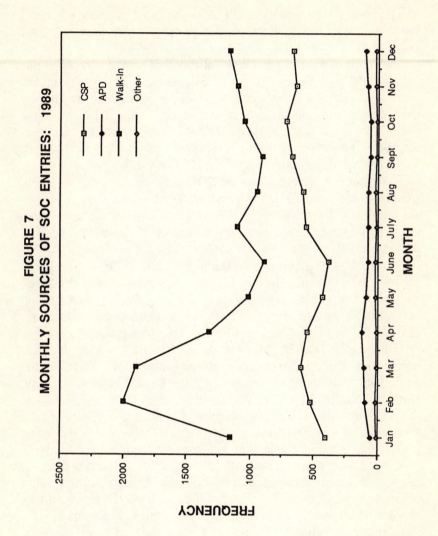

FIGURE 7
MONTHLY SOURCES OF SOC ENTRIES: 1989

23

ple, or responds to requests by the Anchorage Police Department (APD) to bring drunks to the SOC.

Transport to the SOC by APD was the other primary source of entry, followed by a few people per month coming directly from a hospital or other sources.

The shape of the walk-in curve follows that for the admission rate as a whole (see Figure 2). The CSP admissions show slight increases when the walk-in curve starts to decline, which was during early spring and late summer months. APD appeared to be transporting about the same number of people a month to the SOC during 1989, but their transports also showed a slight increase between February and April, with a leveling off afterward.

The nature of the entries to the SOC indicates that it was largely used by homeless walk-ins in varied states of intoxication. The people brought to the SOC by the CSP were clearly intoxicated, which implies that such entries were too intoxicated to make it to the SOC by themselves, as were those transported by the police.

Figure 8 is a graphic representation of total SOC admission sources. Bean's Cafe, Brother Francis Shelter (BFS) and the SOC, are located within a short distance of each other in a compound about three-quarters of a mile from the downtown area, easily accessible by walking. Many people thus congregate within the compound to eat at Bean's Cafe, rest or sleep at BFS (which does not accept intoxicated individuals), and sleep at the SOC. Traffic in the compound consists of rotating among the three facilities. The low number from Bean's under-represents the number of walk-ins from there because they were logged as just walk-ins. Regardless, the congregation of people in the compound represented a gathering place for the homeless and transients that accounted for many of SOC's walk-in cases. The CSP accounted for the second largest proportion, totally comprised of the public inebriate population who consistently used the SOC. The Anchorage Police Department was another major source of admissions. The Police, when the CSP is unavailable, or when they find intoxicated persons away from the downtown area, or when called to hospitals to "pick-up" intoxicated persons, or when responding to calls to private residences, usually transport intoxicated persons directly to the SOC unless another disposition is warranted (e.g., jail, hospital). It is not unusual

FIGURE 8
TOTAL SOC ENTRY SOURCES: 1989

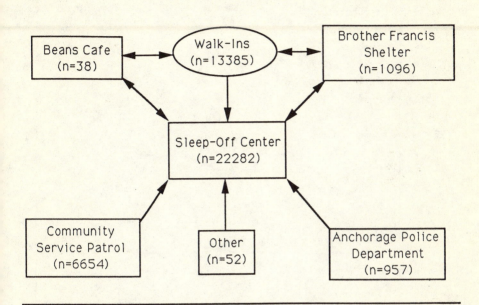

for the police to return to a hospital to retransport a person to the SOC after aid was administered. Thus the source of referrals, in many instances, actually represented a selected combination of agencies that ultimately resulted in persons taken to the SOC.

Figure 9 provides a comparison of the first quarter data for sources of entry for 1989 and 1990 for the three major entry modalities (CSP, APD and Walk-in). The APD referrals remained similar, but a reverse of the 1989 entries took place in 1990 regarding walkins, as shown by a decline in February 1990, followed by an increase in March, a trend consistent with the total entry data (see Figure 7). The CSP entries increase in 1990 compared to 1989, which indicates that fewer people were walking in and relying more on the CSP for transport to the SOC, perhaps because of increased intoxication.

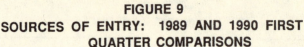

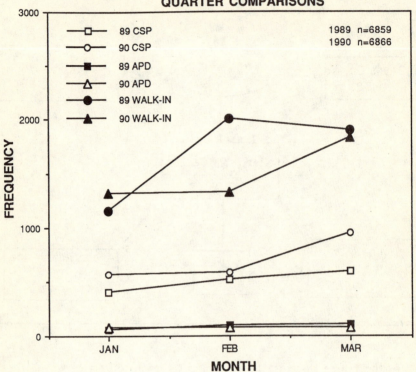

(2) Residential Status

The residential status of those who entered the SOC during 1989 appears in Figure 10. These data represent responses to the question of whether one had a "regular" place to stay. The predominate response was homeless (94.3%); the other responses represented where people said they had recently resided. (Out of state and out of town were defined as being in Anchorage less than two weeks.)

A comparison of the first quarter residential status of 1989 and 1990 revealed that homeless status increased slightly. Homelessness was reported by 98.3 percent of the cases in 1990, compared with 95.9 percent in the first quarter of 1989. The remainder of the

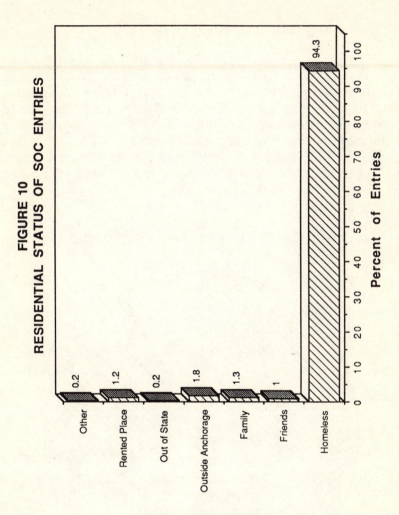

FIGURE 10
RESIDENTIAL STATUS OF SOC ENTRIES

Other 0.2
Rented Place 1.2
Out of State 0.2
Outside Anchorage 1.8
Family 1.3
Friends 1
Homeless 94.3

Residential Status

Percent of Entries

27

entry sources were comparable during the first quarters of 1989 and 1990.

(3) Entry Condition

Shown in Figure 11 are the results of an assessment of the client's condition by intake staff on entry to the SOC. As is clearly illustrated, the most frequent condition was alcohol intoxication (88.51%). A few people (8.29%) entered without apparent signs of having used alcohol or other drugs. Less than one percent were recorded as having been under the influence of a drug other than alcohol (0.8%), and 2.4 percent mixed alcohol and other drugs. These data show that the SOC clearly served as a shelter for public inebriates to sleep-off their intoxication.

FIGURE 11
CONDITION OF CLIENTS ON ENTRY TO SOC

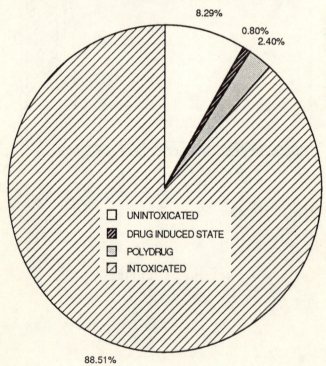

8.29%

0.80%
2.40%

UNINTOXICATED
DRUG INDUCED STATE
POLYDRUG
INTOXICATED

88.51%

Analysis of the first quarter data for 1990 showed that the proportion of the intoxicated increased compared to 1989, with 89.4 percent of the cases reported as entering in a staggering condition in 1990, compared to 57.2 percent in the first quarter of 1989.

(4) Length of Stay

The length of time people stayed at the SOC is shown in Figure 12. The mean length of stay was 6.2 hours. The highest proportion of people remained an hour or less. The most frequent length of stay ranged from four to ten hours. Many people left soon after entry for meals, after which they returned to the SOC or drifted back downtown, only to return later.

(5) Departure Sources

The effect of the three shelters/agencies (SOC, Bean's and BFS) close together in the same compound is noticeable in the departure statistics described in Figure 13. Departure to Bean's and BFS account for a combined total of 63.7 percent of the places where clients said they were going after leaving the SOC. Many people also returned directly to the street on exiting the SOC. Three percent (3.0%) of the client population during the year were referred to a hospital. Just under 2 percent (1.8%) went into detox. Some were arrested and escorted by the police to jail for protective custody or for criminal charges (1.0%), while the remainder either went to work, back home or to a friend or relative (2.5%). Most of the people who entered, however, eventually went back to the street after eating at Bean's or resting at BFS. Many displaced people drifted between the SOC, BFS and Bean's, which accounted for the high number of entries and short stay by some consistent SOC users.

In summarizing the entry data, the SOC was chiefly used by homeless street people who arrived largely by walking in. The SOC's location next to the BFS and Bean's Cafe contributed in large part to the number of walk-ins. The nonambulatory intoxicated were transported either by the CSP or APD. Most cases stayed within the SOC-Bean's-BFS compound after leaving the SOC.

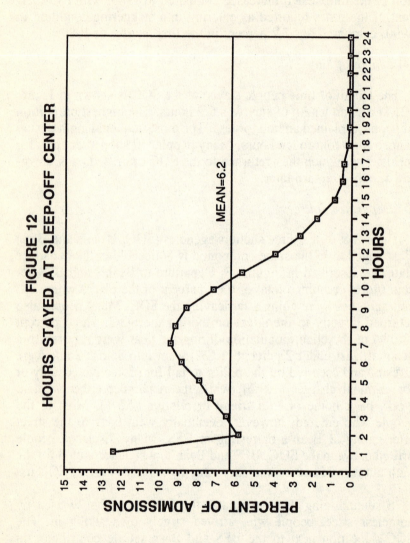

FIGURE 12
HOURS STAYED AT SLEEP-OFF CENTER

MEAN=6.2

PERCENT OF ADMISSIONS

HOURS

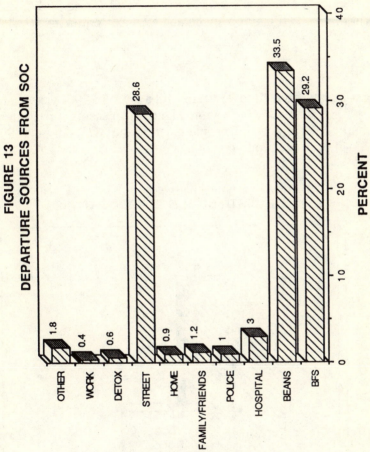

FIGURE 13
DEPARTURE SOURCES FROM SOC

31

C. Demographics

(1) Gender

Of the 22,282 duplicate entries to the SOC during 1989, 12.9 percent (n = 2,872) were women and 87.1 percent (n = 19,419) were men.

(2) Age

Ages ranged from 18 to 85 years with a mean of 39.4 years (median = 38 yrs; mode = 38 yrs). Figure 14 presents a frequency distribution of the ages[1] of people entering the SOC during 1989. The 35-44 year age group predominate, followed by the 25-34 age

FIGURE 14
AGE DISTRIBUTION OF SOC ENTRIES

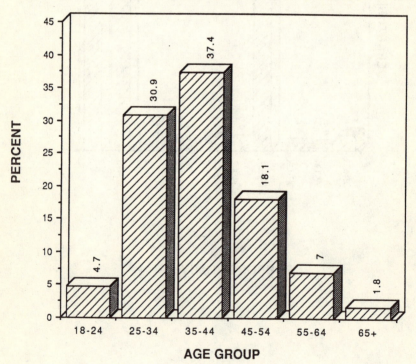

group. Collectively, over a quarter of the entries (26.9%) were 45 years or older.

Figure 15 identifies the mean age distribution by month. The mean age was generally younger (below the mean) during the early months of operation, but after March the monthly mean entry age increased (above the mean) and remained high after that, and then dropped moderately after September.

These changes reflect both seasonal variation and use of the SOC by predominately older people after March. In the winter people stay in Anchorage waiting for warmer weather. During this layover it is not uncommon to drink and to use public facilities. As spring and summer approach many younger people leave for fishing and other seasonal jobs. During the fall they begin to return to Anchorage to "winter over." The upward slope of the curve after October reflects this change. Overall, however, it appears that the changes in the age curve reflect the fact that the SOC was used by older public inebriates after March.

(3) Ethnicity

The SOC clientele consisted mostly of Alaskan Natives, who constituted 74.3 percent of the entries (see Figure 16). The term "Alaskan Native" is a composite representing an Alaskan-born indigenous person who is either Inupiat (28.7%) or Yupik Eskimo (16.4%), Athabascan Indian (14.3%), Tlingit (5.3%) or Haida Indian (16.4%), or Aleut (9.4%).

The other predominate racial group was White (20.3%). Other ethnic groups comprised a total of 5.4 percent, consisting of Blacks (1.7%), American Indians (2.4%), Hispanics (0.6%) and Asian-Pacific Islanders (0.4%). Those not identifiable or from another group constituted only 0.3% percent of the population.

Figure 17 shows a breakdown of ethnicity by gender. Alaskan Native males were the most frequent SOC users, followed by White males. Women SOC users were mostly Alaskan Native or White.

Figure 18 shows DSC entries by month and race, grouped into three ethnic categories (Alaskan Native, White, and Other, representing a combination of all other racial groups). The Alaskan Na-

FIGURE 15
AVERAGE ENTRY AGE BY MONTH

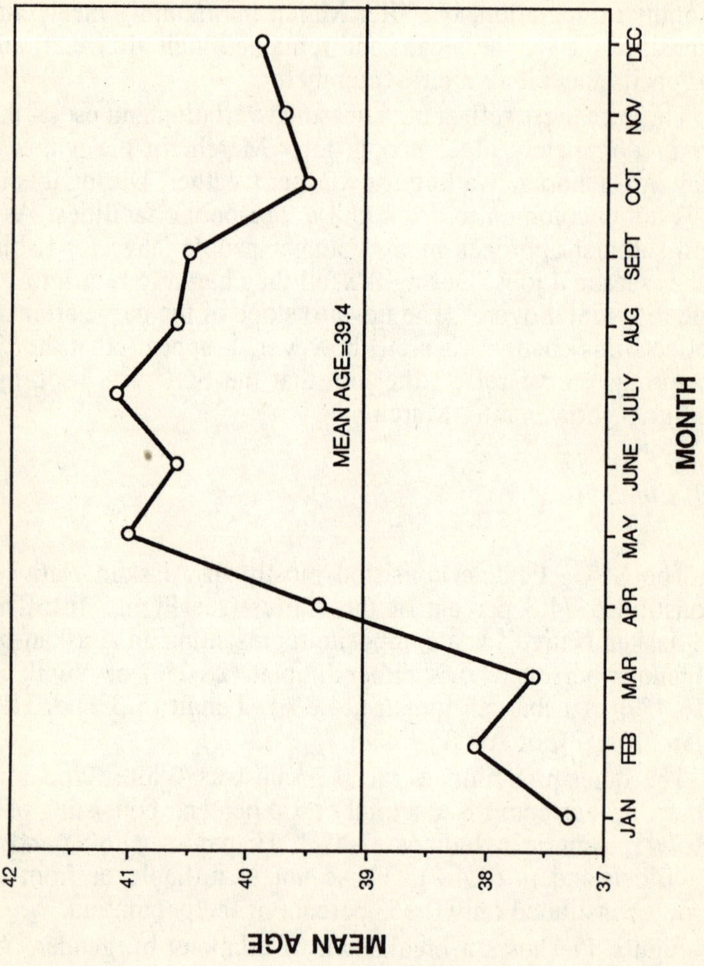

MEAN AGE=39.4

MEAN AGE

MONTH

34

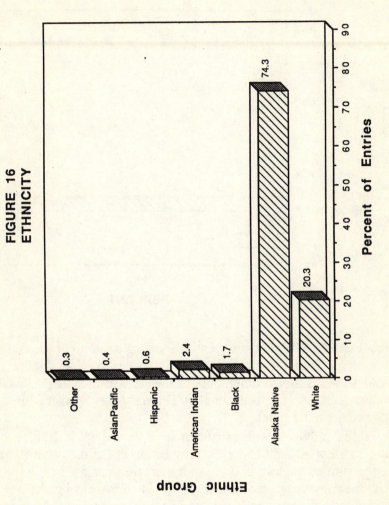

FIGURE 16
ETHNICITY

35

FIGURE 17
ETHNICITY AND GENDER

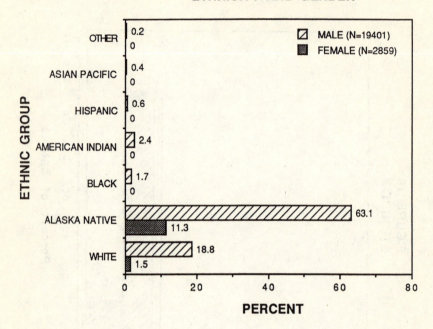

tives used the SOC most frequently, showing a pattern of use that is isomorphic with the monthly use pattern described in Figure 2. Whites show a similar trend, but of a lower magnitude than Alaskan Natives. Except for a decline in February the "Other" group showed a similar trend.

Table 2 provides a comparison of some demographic data for the first quarters of 1989 and 1990. Inspection of the data shows that gender shifted slightly in that use by females increased (+3.8%), while use by males decreased (−3.8%). Those using the SOC tended to be younger, reflected by the mean age declining by over a year (−1.3 yrs.). Ethnic representation also changed. Alaskan Natives tended to use it more (+15.1%), while Whites (−9.6%) and Blacks (−3.9%) entered less, as did Hispanics, (−1.1%), Asian-Pacific Islanders (−0.1%) and Others (−0.15).

FIGURE 18
MONTHLY ENTRY BY ETHNIC GROUP

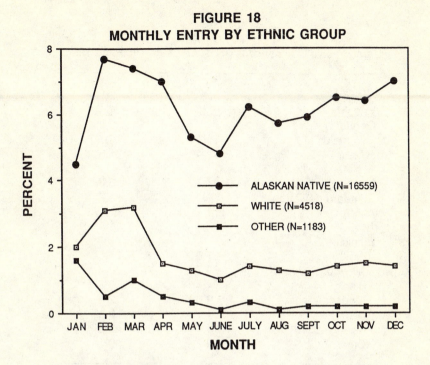

D. *Blood Alcohol Level (BAL)*

Each client's blood alcohol level (BAL), as noted earlier, was assessed upon entry to the SOC. This was done to identify people at risk because of extraordinarily high BALs, and also to monitor drinking behavior. People with BALs over 0.30, were carefully watched or referred to a hospital emergency room. The measurement of the blood alcohol level provided a unique opportunity to learn about the drinking behavior of street people or the public inebriate.

(1) BAL and Admissions

Figure 19 shows the average number of admissions per month and the average monthly BAL for 1989. As admissions decreased, the BAL increased. The mean BAL for the year was 0.190, and the

Table 2

Demographic Comparisons: First Quarters 1989 and 1990

	Percent	
Variable	1989	1990
Gender		
Female	10.6	14.4
Male	89.4	85.6
Mean Age	37.7	39.0
Standard deviation	9.7	9.7
Age Range	18 to 85	18 to 76
Ethnicity		
White	27.0	17.4
Alaskan Native	63.7	78.8
Black	4.4	0.5
American Indian	2.6	2.6
Hispanic	1.1	0.0
Asian-Pacific	1.0	0.0
Other	0.2	0.1

mean of the means for monthly BALs was 0.174. Not only was a high BAL level maintained, but this was associated with ongoing intoxication. Seventy-seven percent of the entries were described as having "staggered in," and 4.3 percent needed assistance to enter.

In April, admissions to the SOC decreased while drinking increased, and was maintained at a moderately high level. People using the SOC were remaining intoxicated while on the street, with the SOC becoming a shelter primarily for the intoxicated people. Client characteristics were different prior to April when many younger and sober people used the facility to get out of the cold. When the admission policy changed, as discussed previously, the composition of the people using the SOC also changed. The ongoing SOC users clearly shifted to the older public inebriate.

The average mean monthly BAL of .174 implies that at any given time, someone who used the SOC had consumed enough alcohol to be at least moderately intoxicated.

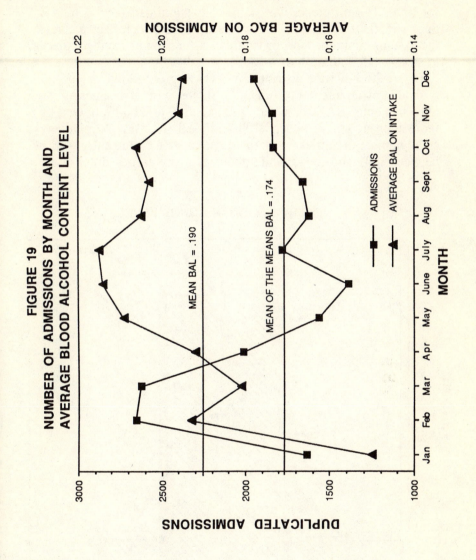

FIGURE 19
NUMBER OF ADMISSIONS BY MONTH AND
AVERAGE BLOOD ALCOHOL CONTENT LEVEL

39

A comparison of the entry BALs for the first quarters of 1989 and 1990, revealed that the mean BAL for 1989 was 0.149, and 0.258 for 1990. This difference was statistically significant ($t = -62.95$, df $= 9650$, $p < .001$). The increase appears to reflect a direct increase in drinking, most probably as a function of having a place to sleep while intoxicated.

Figure 20 shows the distribution of BALs grouped into categories separated by an interval of 0.09. The majority of those entering the SOC had entry BALs between .100 and .190 (44.1%) followed by those with a BAL between .200 and .290 (42.5%). A relatively small number of entries drank to a lesser degree before entry (4.8% between .001 and .099) while about as many entries drank more

FIGURE 20
ENTRY BLOOD ALCOHOL LEVELS

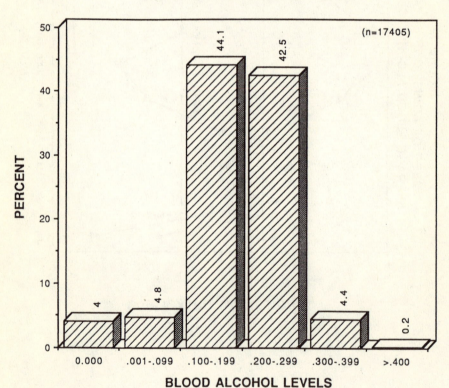

extensively (BAL > .300 = 4.6%). Only 4 percent of the entries during the year did not register any detectable alcohol intake when their BAL was taken.

(2) Blood Alcohol Level and Gender

BAL by gender is shown in Figure 21. Overall, males maintained higher BALs than females.

Figure 22 shows BAL and gender within each of the BAL groups. Males were consistently higher than females.

(3) Blood Alcohol Level and Ethnicity

The characterization of the SOC population during 1989 by ethnic group and BALs obtained by members of different ethnic groups are presented in Figure 23. Alaskan Natives, who constituted the largest number of SOC users, showed the highest proportion of intoxication with BALs registering between 0.100 and 0.299. A smaller percentage of Alaskan Natives also obtained BALs greater than 0.300.

Figure 24 shows the percent of persons *within* each ethnic group who entered the SOC classified by BAL. All groups had members who drank heavily, but the smallest proportion of heavy drinking was found among Blacks, Hispanics, and Asian-Pacific Islanders (ASAINPAC). Alaskan Natives and American Indians showed the highest levels of intoxication, represented by BALs ranging between 0.100 and 0.299. There also was a consistent representation of Whites and members of the "Other" group who maintained a BAL between 0.100 and 0.199. Whites also tended to have representation in the higher BAL categories.

Ethnic representation *within* each of the BAL groups is shown in Figure 25. The pattern of drinking represented in Figure 25 shows that Alaskan Natives maintained a disproportionally high alcohol intake in comparison with the other ethnic groups. Inspection of the data shows that there is representation of the different ethnic groups within the lower BAL range (0.001 to 0.099), but as the BAL increases, ethnic representation shifts toward the Alaskan Native.

Figure 26 presents the relationship between BAL and ethnicity, showing the percent of *ethnic representation within blood alcohol*

FIGURE 21
BAL BY GENDER

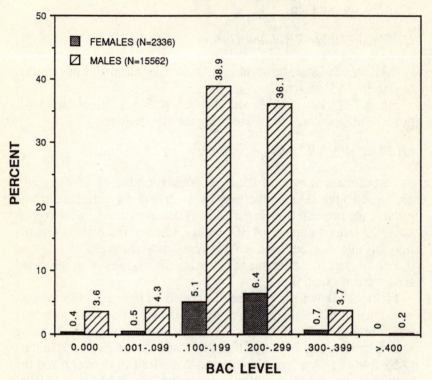

levels. What is most noticeable is that while drinking (decreasing BALs within each group) declines for the White, Black, Hispanic and Asian-Pacific-Islanders, drinking (rising BALs within the group) increases dramatically for the Alaskan Native. The American Indian group shows about an equal number of drinkers between 0.001 and 0.399, but there is a rise in the number of people who drank at a level greater than 0.400.

A comparison of BALs on entry by ethnic groups (White, Alaskan Native, and Others) for the first quarters of 1989 and 1990 is shown in Figure 27. The difference between the BAL levels for 1989 and 1990 was statistically significant for all three groups.

In summary of the ethnic-BAL data, there is a clear indication of

FIGURE 22
BAL AND GENDER WITHIN BAL GROUPS

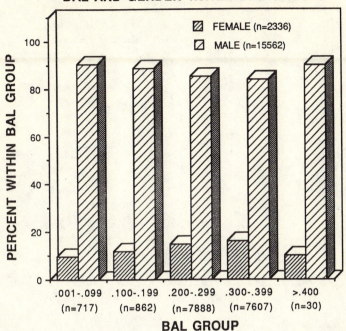

intoxication among Alaskan Natives who used the SOC. Although other ethnic groups manifested heavy drinking, their levels were lower than Alaskan Natives. A Chi Square test of significance of the data pertaining to BAL and ethnicity yielded a value of 3203, which was statistically significant (df $= 30, p < .001$), indicating that there is a relationship between alcohol consumption and ethnicity.

The BAL data suggests that drinking by SOC users was not only continuous, but that high BALs were more the norm than the exception. People were repeatedly intoxicated and used the SOC as a place to sleep off their drunkenness. Moreover, they negotiated between the SOC, BFS and Bean's or roamed the streets while intoxicated. When highly intoxicated they could count on the police or CSP to get them to the SOC. This overall arrangement most probably contributed to the increase in drinking in the first quarter of

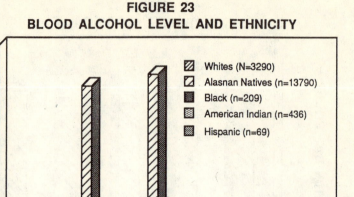

FIGURE 23
BLOOD ALCOHOL LEVEL AND ETHNICITY

1990. Given the ostensibly sheltered environment in which the public inebriate functioned there apparently was little motivation or incentive to curtail drinking. Additionally, the change in policy after March, 1989, may also have helped to shift the client population to heavy drinking street people.

Additionally, in examining the finding that Alaskan Natives showed extremely high BALs, representative of heavy drinking and intoxication, the question arises as to what contributes to this exceptionally high rate of drinking among the Alaskan Native.

One factor that may contribute to this excessive drinking is the urban environment itself. Studies contrasting urban and rural American Indians found marked differences in drinking behavior between members of these two communities. Urban residents drank more heavily and had a lower rate of abstainers when compared to rural counterparts (Young, 1988). Graves (1971), in one of the pio-

FIGURE 24
BAL WITHIN ETHNIC GROUPS

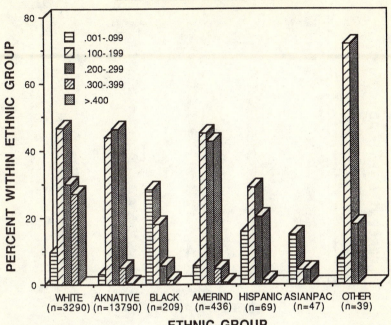

neer studies of drinking behavior among urban American Indians, concluded that elevated drinking among a population of urban American Indians "can be understood in light of the fact that their preparation for successful, unstressful urban living is far poorer [in comparison to other, urban-oriented ethnic groups]" (p. 306). According to Graves, a major influence underlying heavy drinking is that it serves as a means of coping with feelings of personal inadequacy and failure by temporarily escaping from them. The same circumstances can be generalized to the Alaskan Native finding her/himself in Anchorage.

Another factor which has been described as contributing to heavy drinking among Native Americans is cultural practice or traditions. Heavy binge drinking among Native Americans may represent the cultural practice of consuming all the alcohol that is available or to drink until drunk in a group setting (Heath, 1989; Young, 1988).

FIGURE 25
ETHNICITY AND BAL WITHIN BAL GROUP

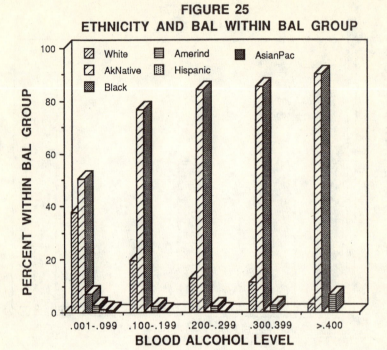

Drinking behavior is perceived as behavior that is expected and sanctioned within a particular drinking context or even as a cultural characteristic. Drinking what is available, or what is offered, is an important manifestation of this cultural tradition. When one has no alcohol available, he/she is welcomed and expected to drink among those drinking, and the person is expected to share his/her alcohol when others have none to drink. Even when one wants to refrain from drinking the influence of the drinking group is sufficiently strong so that the person will succumb to the expected behavior and drink along with the others (Andre, 1979). This "sharing" characteristic, which is an important part of Alaskan Native Cultures, no doubt contributes to the group drinking that is seen along the avenue, and to the high levels of intoxication recorded among the drinking Native street people.

Use of a cultural explanation such as sharing to account for binge drinking among Native American populations has been a focus of

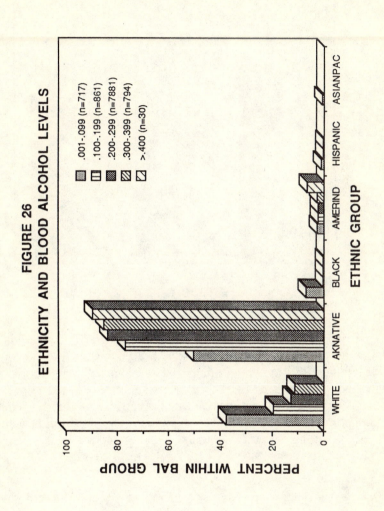

FIGURE 26
ETHNICITY AND BLOOD ALCOHOL LEVELS

.001-.099 (n=717)
.100-.199 (n=861)
.200-.299 (n=7881)
.300-.399 (n=794)
>.400 (n=30)

PERCENT WITHIN BAL GROUP

ETHNIC GROUP

WHITE   AKNATIVE   BLACK   AMERIND   HISPANIC   ASIANPAC

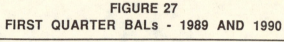

FIGURE 27
FIRST QUARTER BALs - 1989 AND 1990

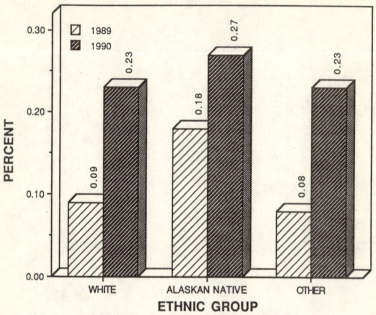

much research, which resulted in its being interpreted as a unique "Indian" style that is the "most easily observed and exotic" (May, 1977). But while American Indians and Alaskan Natives do contain many people who drink markedly more than others in the population, abstainers and other types of drinkers can also be found. Heath (1989) points out that recent research has found such significant variations among American Indian drinking practices that "any broad generalization is suspect" (p. 209). Heath goes on to say that:

the stenotype of spectacular binge drinking among Indians is well established, not only in folklore but also in a number of apparently authoritative sources. However, it is more than an ethnographic curiosity that there is virtually no drinking among many other Indian populations. A similar example is the fact that most studies of Indian drinking have focused on drinking among men, who have been found to drink more, and more often than Indian women. (p. 209)

May (1989) indicated that:

the styles of consumption among Indian drinkers result in both alcohol-related and alcohol-specific problems. It should again be pointed out . . . that a bulk of these statistics is produced by a minority of Indians and that many Indians abstain or drink without problems. Many Indian drinkers never get into accidents or get arrested. In fact, to a greater degree than with other adults in the United States, a great number of Indians quit drinking after age 30. Unfortunately, some of those who do drink become casualties before they quit or change from a flamboyant, recreational style of consumption. (pp. 113-114)

While it is not possible to account for drinking solely as a function of cultural influence, culture nevertheless plays a role, one which is more decisive regarding the social interaction among drinkers than the drinking behavior itself. It seems that drinking is more of a recreational behavior that has become a prominent feature of the urban scene for Native Americans (Graves, 1971). This social process may also apply to the heavily drinking nonnative SOC users. The research issue thus becomes one of unearthing the role that social and other factors have in determining the kinds of drinking and alcohol-related behaviors that occur within given populations.

Another factor considered to be related to drinking among American Native groups is biological influences. Significant attention in recent years in the form of family, twin, adoption and genetic studies, has been directed at the examination of the role that heredity plays in the etiology of alcoholism (Cloninger, 1987; Goodwin, 1988; Li & Bosron, 1986). The results of this research has led to the concept of a "biological vulnerability" to alcoholism. This concept has recently been reinforced by the discovery of different levels of sensitivity and adverse reactions and possible liver diseases among individuals of different racial or ethnic groups (Goedde et al., 1989; Schuckit, 1987; Shibuya & Yoshida, 1989; Singh et al., 1989; Zeiner, 1980). It has been found, for example, that a higher percentage of people of Asian ancestry (e.g., Chinese, Japanese, Koreans, etc.) in general, as well as Northern, Southwestern and Western Plains Indians metabolize alcohol more rapidly than non-Asians (Goedde & Agarwal, 1990). This difference is believe to be primarily related to differences in alcohol dehydrogenase (ADH) and in aldehyde dehydrogenase polymorphisms (ALDH) (Goedde et al., 1989). It has also been reported that a high percentage of Asians experience an excessive accumulation of acetaldehyde due to a deficiency in the low K_m isoenzyme form of aldehyde dehydrogenase (Goedde et al., 1989). Specifically, about 50% of the Asian group showed an undue accumulation of acetaldehyde, seemingly attributable to a relatively inefficient or completely inefficient variant of aldehyde dehydrogenase (ALDH) (Goedde et al., 1989).

The blocking of enzymatic degradation of acetaldehyde results in very unpleasant side effects after alcohol consumption, such as facial flushing, an increase in heart rate, palpitations, tachycardia, muscle weakness, and headaches. This strong aversive reaction has been interpreted as protecting people who have this form of aldehyde dehydrogenase deficiency from becoming alcoholic (Thomasson et al., 1989a, 1989b; Nagoshi et al., 1988; Yoshida, Wang, & Dave, 1983). Additionally, there appears to be differences among racial groups in the allelic frequency of alcohol dehydrogenase (ADH).

It has been hypothesized that the alcohol flush reaction is, to a large degree, a function of the genotype of the individual having this newly detected inborn error of metabolism, called the ALDH deficiency (Goedde & Agarwal, 1989). Since alcohol is believed to be metabolized differently in different racial groups due to differences in alcohol dehydrogenase (ADH) activity, it is likely that differences in alcohol dehydrogenase and aldehyde dehydrogenase alleles may contribute to the drinking pattern found among Alaskan Natives and American Indians. This assumption is in need of further research.

No single explanation, however, can account for why drinking behavior was so exceedingly high among Alaskan Natives. The level of drinking observed was sufficiently high and consistent to indicate that many of the SOC admissions are drinking alcoholically. Drinking for such individuals would thus revolve around a need to drink, typical of the alcoholic. If a large percent of those with persistently high BALs are drinking alcoholically, their drinking, which may have started as a form of binge drinking, or even recreational drinking, has progressed to steady-state drinking. These people use the SOC as a respite while they continue to drink. The task becomes one of determining how to intervene effectively, with less of a focus on determining the reasons for drinking.

One direct implication of the continued high alcohol intake, as evidenced by the steady rate of elevated BALs, is the eventual onset of drinking-related health problems and an exacerbation of current social problems. Acutely high blood-alcohol levels have been associated with alcohol-related arrests, death and illness. Thus alcohol-related mortality from cirrhosis of the liver and other alcohol-related diseases, from accidents and other alcohol-related causes will increase. Additionally, alcohol-related arrests and detentions, violence, and other alcohol-related problems, will also intensify over time. Indeed, during 1989 and 1990 at least 24 alcohol-related deaths of known street people have occurred, some violently.

(4) Number of Entries and Average BAL

The number of entries per person and average BAL per person on entry is shown in Figure 28. The pattern of admission observed was that people with BALs between 0.100 and 0.199 used the SOC less frequently than people with higher BALs. Conversely, those with higher BALs used the SOC more frequently. The pattern of SOC use shown in Figure 28 is consistent with the findings cited above which indicated that the SOC primarily served as a shelter for highly intoxicated persons.

(5) Age and BAL

Figure 29 provides data on age and BAL. Drinking occurred across all age groups, but those between 25 and 54 years drank most heavily, with BALS ranging between 0.100 and 0.299. This level of drinking also extended to people between 55 and 64 years, but to a lesser extent. Those between 25-44 years, however, showed a tendency to drink fairly consistently within BALs ranging from 0.100 to 0.299.

FIGURE 28
NUMBER OF ENTRIES AND AVERAGE BAL PER PERSON

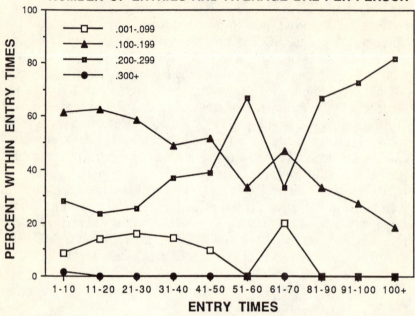

The pattern of drinking shown in Figure 29 is consistent with data projecting alcohol consumption in the United States (Williams et al., 1987). In their projections, Williams et al., forecast that the 21-34 age group would show the highest level of consumption, followed by the 35-49 year-old group. The drinking pattern which emerged in this study is very consistent with this prediction.

A description of the level of intoxication *within age groups* is shown in Figure 30. These data reveal that the youngest group were less intoxicated in relation to older groups. Beginning with age 25, and extending up to 54 years, however, there was about an equal proportion of people who achieved consistently high BALs. Drinking, for many of those using the SOC between these age brackets, was fairly consistent. After age 54 there was a sharp increase in the proportion of people achieving a BAL between 0.100 and 0.199, and a decrease in those who drank heavier. Those above 65 years, in contrast showed a small decline in moderate drinking (between

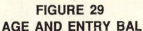

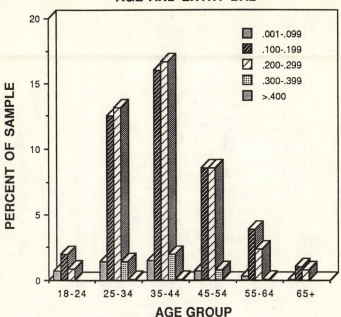

FIGURE 29
AGE AND ENTRY BAL

0.100 and 0.199) and a slight increase in heavier drinking (>
0.200).

Figure 31 shows the relationship between average monthly age
on entering the SOC and average monthly BAL. As the average age
is increased, the level of drinking increased correspondingly. The
relationship between age and drinking level is linear, as represented
by a Pearson correlation coefficient of .87 (df = 10, p < .01). As
the SOC continued to function over the year the number of admissions increased, as did the level of drinking among the entries.

The age-BAL data is also fairly uniform when comparing drinking problems among homeless adults in American cities, as shown
in Figure 32. Using an annual average BAL cut point of > =0.100
to indicate problem drinking, a comparison was made with data
pertaining to problem drinking among homeless adults in 16 U.S.
cities by Wright et al. (1987). The data for the study by Wright et

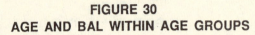

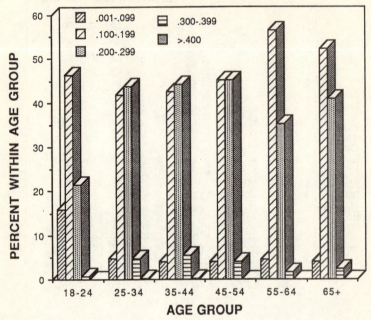

FIGURE 30
AGE AND BAL WITHIN AGE GROUPS

al. used a younger age group of 16-29, which was not comparable to our data, in which the youngest age begins at 18.

The rate of drinking for males in the 18-29 age group are reasonably close, but the Anchorage women show a rate of problem drinking about three times higher than the comparison groups. Additionally, the Anchorage men and women in the 30-49 age group revealed much higher levels of what has been described as problem drinking. Women in particular demonstrated a level of problem drinking three times greater than those in the comparison group.

As age increases the overall proportion of problem drinking decreases more sharply for women than for men. The Anchorage men, in comparison to their counterparts in the 50-64 and 65+ age groups, showed much lower levels of problem drinking. The Anchorage women within the 50-64 age group are slightly lower than their counterparts, but they are slightly higher within the 65+ group.

FIGURE 31
AVERAGE MONTHY AGE AND AVERAGE MONTHLY BAL

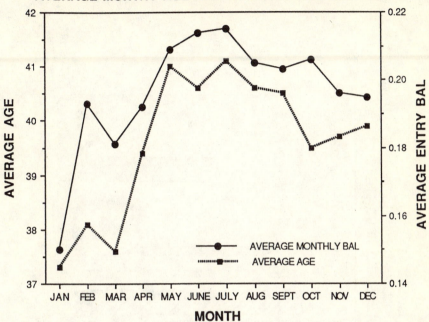

In summary of the age data, there is a clear relationship between homeless men and women, age and drinking behavior. Specifically, as age increases alcohol consumption increases, but after about age 65 the level begins to decline. In the United States the pattern is for alcohol abuse to be highest among the young and to decline generally with age (Wright et al., 1987), a pattern evidenced in the data reported herein. A Chi Square test of significance of the contingency table for the data for age and BAL yielded a coefficient of 793.86, which was statistically significant (df $= 25$, $p <$ .001), indicating that there is a relationship between drinking levels across age groups, that is, drinking is not independent of age.

The high proportion of drinking found during the middle years raises the question of whether drinking at this stage of one's life cycle is a reflection of homelessness (i.e., coping), or whether homelessness is a consequence of drinking. Whatever the reason,

FIGURE 32
COMPARISON OF DRINKING AMONG HOMELESS MEN AND WOMEN: ANCHORAGE AND 16 US CITIES

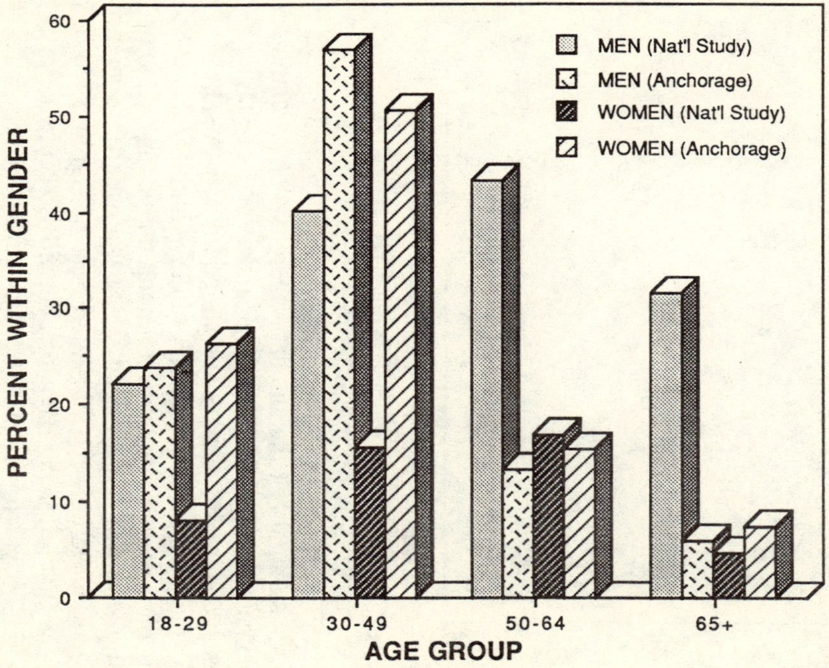

PERCENT WITHIN GENDER
0
10
20
30
40
50
60
MEN (Nat'l Study)
MEN (Anchorage)
WOMEN (Nat'l Study)
WOMEN (Anchorage)
18-29
30-49
50-64
65+
AGE GROUP

heavy drinking within the middle years cuts across ethnicity and gender, and places these individuals at high risk for adverse health and social problems.

(6) Entry Source and BAL

Figure 33 shows the relationship between BAL and entry source. Both the Community Service Patrol (CSP) and the Anchorage Police Department (APD) transported the same proportion of intoxicated people to the SOC with BALs between 0.100 and 0.299, and greater than 0.300. Many people walked in with BALs between 0.100 and 0.199. Those with higher BALs also managed to walk in, but were more likely to be admitted via CSP or APD.

FIGURE 33
ENTRY SOURCE AND BLOOD ALCOHOL LEVEL

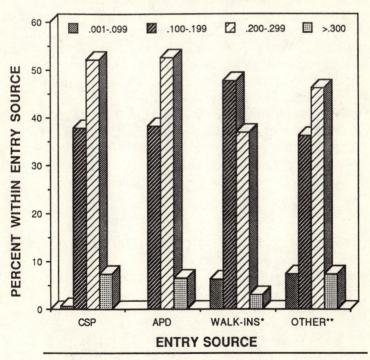

*Includes walk-ins from the street, BFS and Beans.
**Includes walk-ins from hospitals and other community facilities.

(7) Time at SOC by BAL

Shown in Figure 34 is the relationship between the length of time in hours spent at the SOC and BAL. The data is consistent with that discussed above which indicates that many people entering the SOC were intoxicated, chiefly represented by BALs between 0.100 and 0.299. The data also shows that the higher the BAL (> 0.299) the longer the stay.

In summary of the utilization data, there is a clear pattern of use to indicate that SOC developed into a shelter primarily serving intoxicated people. At its inception the SOC catered to large numbers of people seeking shelter, whether intoxicated or not. As the SOC developed its policies, and as the season began to change from winter to spring, use of the SOC evolved into a steady clientele of homeless public inebriates who drank steadily, with some transients, and some who needed temporary shelter, using the SOC apparently on an as-need basis. The frequent user group consisted largely of Alaskan Natives (74.3%), and males (63.1%). A fifth of the entries were White (20.3%) of whom 18.8 percent were males.

The next section analyzes the data in terms of unduplicated entries during 1989, that is, identifies individuals regardless of their number of entries. This analysis permits a more definitive exploration of the characteristics of the street population. The unduplicated and duplicated statistics, it should be noted, will always remain in a constant proportion to one another. Any variation in individual statistics may have resulted from cases being deleted due to missing values for any of the variables used in statistical analyses.

PART II.
UNDUPLICATED CLIENT CHARACTERISTICS: 1989

A. Demographics

(1) Gender and Age

The 22,282 cases who used the SOC during 1989 consisted of 1,749 individuals, of which 81 percent ($n = 1416$) were men, and 19 percent were women ($n = 333$). The age distribution, parallels the age distribution described in Part I, is show in Figure 35. The

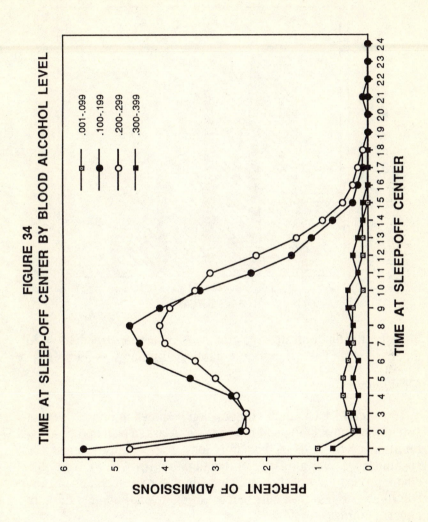

FIGURE 34

TIME AT SLEEP-OFF CENTER BY BLOOD ALCOHOL LEVEL

.001-.099
.100-.199
.200-.299
.300-.399

PERCENT OF ADMISSIONS

TIME AT SLEEP-OFF CENTER

59

FIGURE 35
UNDUPLICATED ENTRIES BY AGE GROUP

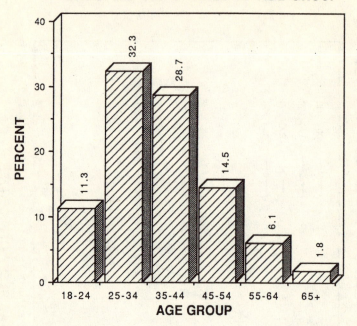

mean for the unduplicated age group was 37.1 years (median = 35; mode = 35). (The mean for the duplicated group was 39.4 yrs.)

(2) Ethnicity

The unduplicated ethnic composition is shown in Figure 36. Consistent with the overall number of entries, Alaskan Natives accounted for almost two-thirds of the admissions, followed by Whites, who encompassed over a quarter of the admissions (27.6%). The other ethnic groups did not show nearly as high a representation, having contributed to less than nine percent of the overall number of unduplicated entries.

(3) Ethnicity and Gender

A breakdown of the ethnic composition by gender (within ethnic group) is shown in Figure 37. Alaskan Native males (82.6%) and females (60.4%) dominated, followed by White males (30.6%) and

FIGURE 36
UNDUPLICATED ENTRIES BY ETHNICITY

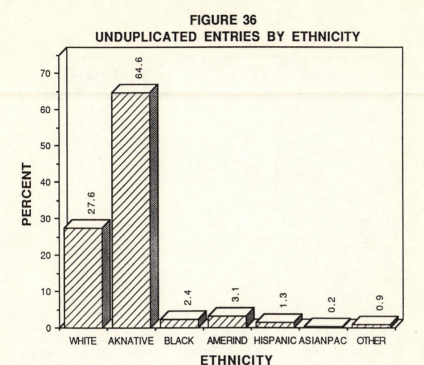

females (14.3%). The other groups showed proportionally less representation.

(4) Gender and Age

Figure 38 reports the proportion of men and women within age groups. The relative proportion of males to females remained stable across age groups starting with 18-24 years, and stayed at about 4:1. Those between 25-34 constituted the highest number of SOC users, followed by those between 35-44 years. As age increased the number of people within age brackets decreased proportionally.

(5) Age, Ethnicity and Gender

Represented in Figure 39 is the age distribution *within ethnic group* by gender. Males outnumbered females within each ethnic

FIGURE 37
UNDUPLICATED ETHNICITY AND GENDER

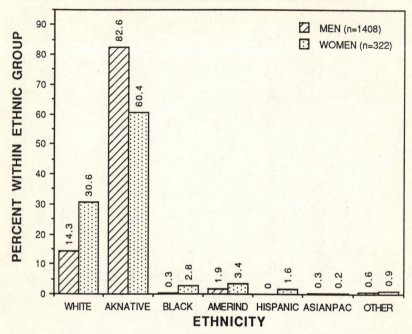

group, which is in keeping with the findings reported earlier. The older SOC users were primarily Alaskan Native of both genders and White males.

The demographic representation of the (unduplicated) SOC population portrays a largely Alaskan Native male and female subgroup who frequented the SOC. White male and females also frequented the SOC, but their representation was smaller than that of the Alaskan Natives.

B. Demographics and Characteristics of Frequent SOC Users

A further analysis of the data on identified those who used the SOC 100 times or more during 1989. Forty-six individuals accounted for more than 100 entries each. Of these, 87 percent (n = 40) were men, 13 percent (n = 6) women. Ages ranged from 20 to

FIGURE 38
UNDUPLICATED GENDER BY AGE GROUP

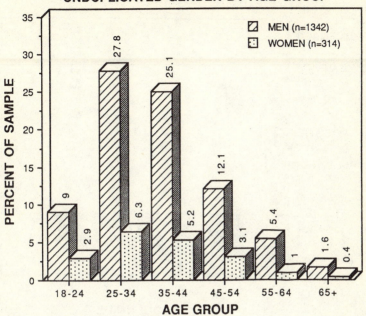

67 years, with a mean age of 39.4 years. (Median and mode = 38 years.) Ethnic composition was: White 8.7 percent, American Indian 2.2 percent, and Alaskan Native 89.1 percent. The average BAL for this group was 0.217, ranging from a low of .167 to a high of .254. A Pearson correlation coefficient, calculated to measure the degree of association between age and number of admissions, yielded a coefficient of −.293 (df = 44, $p < .05$). Although this value is low, it indicates that as age increases the number of admissions tended to decrease. The relationship between age and average BAL yielded a statistically nonsignificant Pearson correlation coefficient of .111 (df = 46, $p > .05$).

In summary, the findings from the unduplicated data indicate that the SOC became a shelter that primarily served older homeless male Alaskan Natives.

The presence of a specific ethnic group constituting a Skid Row

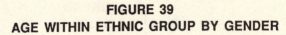

FIGURE 39
AGE WITHIN ETHNIC GROUP BY GENDER

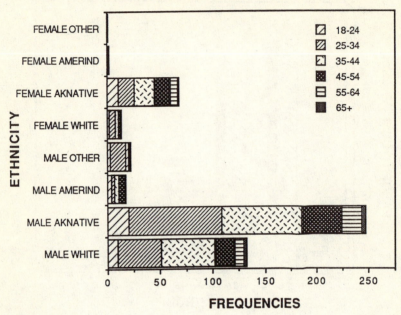

population is not unprecedented. The traditional Skid Row inhabitants of the larger urban centers around the nation were described as "Black and White vagrants of both sexes, especially alcoholic derelicts, who were found to be living in slum areas intermingled with other people" (Blumberg et al., 1978, p. 121). As times change, and the sociological attributes change as the characteristics of cities change, the nature of the Skid Row population changes accordingly. Garrett (1990) reflects that while Skid Row has all but disappeared in American cities, the homeless have not. Skid Row, as Blumberg et al. (1978) stated "is a characteristic of people within our society. It is a complex of poverty, powerlessness, alienation, homelessness, and, perhaps, alcohol or drug addiction, for which we are all eligible to a greater or lesser degree" (pp. 121-122).

In Anchorage, where the Alaskan Native, more than any other ethnic group, has been subject to displacement and acculturation stress (cf., Segal, 1983), and in a dominate culture where minority status and poverty are closely related, it can be expected that there will be a large number of Alaskan Natives who are likely to be Skid Row candidates. For example, Blumberg et al. (1978), in their exploration of Philadelphia's Skid Row population, noted that:

> There is evidence to support the notion that there is a population of Black Skid Row-like people, even though research on this group is very limited. Du Bois's 1899 study, *The Philadelphia Negro* . . . , pointed out that Blacks were over-represented among those arrested by Philadelphia's Vagrant Detectives. Through the last 100 years of Philadelphia's history, there has been a substantial population of Blacks who have been arrested for such typical Skid Row offenses as drunkenness, vagrancy, breach of the peace, and the like. (p. 123)

In Anchorage, a city mostly comprised of Whites, the Alaskan Native, its second largest subgroup, represents a minority population, as do other ethnic groups. The analogy can be made that the Alaskan Native population in Anchorage represents what Blacks symbolize to Whites in other large urban cities. Thus, following the reasoning of Blumberg et al. (1978), one of the factors that may contribute to the large composition of Alaskan Natives among homeless public inebriates is that the dominant White population may simply not expect anything else from the Native population. Thus, the degree to which a self-fulfilling prophecy is at work needs to be explored.

Concerning the pervasive drinking that prevails on the streets, alcohol has always been associated with street life. "It is central to the way Skid Row institutions operate as well as to the stereotype of the general community about Skid Row" (Blumberg et al., 1978, p. 121). Additionally, Skid Row people are essentially powerless people, subject to the power that the environment has over them. The "power" they do experience is obtained from social relationships. The relationships established on the streets sustain a fellowship that introduces an element of structure and consistency, and if drinking is the mutual bonding agent—"so be it."

The pervasiveness of the drinking and homelessness brought to light by this study should not lead to the conclusion that there is a specific "alcohol problem," "homeless problem," or any other type of "problem." Rather, what is happening within Anchorage's Skid Row represents a complex interaction involving alcohol, psychological, social and cultural phenomena, economics, and political factors.

Whatever the cause, there is a significant number of people who have been affected and in turn are impacting the community. The street population has impacted every health and service facility one way or another in connection with their drinking and homeless status. It seems clear that individuals on the street use the system to perpetuate their behavior. This group has the system responding to their immediate situation/condition/needs on demand (and seemingly on their terms).

More specific information about who some of these street people are may help to formulate a better understanding of their current status, and contribute to further an understanding between drinking and homelessness.

NOTE

1. The age intervals were selected by Row Sciences, Inc., the coordination and evaluation agency for the NIAAA Homeless Demonstration Project, to standardize data collection among different projects in several cities conducting research and demonstration studies among the homeless.

Chapter 4

Results and Discussion: Part B. An Analysis of Drinking and Drug-Taking Behavior Among the Homeless

The scientific study of the relationship between alcohol abuse and homelessness has been difficult because of a lack of a clear and systematic definition of homeless. Moreover, "specific information on how many of the homeless experience alcohol-related problems, the nature of these problems, and their relationships to other aspects of homelessness is even more difficult to develop" (Casement, 1987, p. 20). The current research, by monitoring the behavior of a street population, has begun to tie some of this information together by presenting the results from a study of the relationship between drinking (and other forms of drug-taking behavior) and homelessness. The findings however, which are specific to Anchorage, may not be completely applicable to other cities that do not have a comparable population.

Information about homelessness, and other demographic data, were derived from the Initial Screening Inventory (ISI). Before clients left the SOC they were asked to take part in an interview designed to obtain more detailed information about them.

The ISI was administered after the SOC opened, and was given for almost a year. It was stopped because most of those using the SOC were repeaters who were interviewed. Others using the shelter were mostly transients who were not around long enough to complete a questionnaire. The ISI was administered by SOC staff, trained to attain a maximum response rate among hung over, often uncooperative and sometimes combative respondents.

The ISI as pilot tested on over 50 cases during December, 1987, when the SOC was opened on a trial basis. Upon completion of the pilot testing changes were made as necessary to ensure that each question maintained content validity. Reliability was determined by reinterviewing the test cases after the SOC opened formally. Relatively good consistency (78 percent agreement) was obtained.

Information obtained in the interview included demographics, living arrangements, drinking behavior, treatment history, family history, other drug use, and legal status. The ISI alcohol-related questions asking about the quantity of alcohol consumption were designed to be open ended instead of using predefined response categories. For example, the following question was used to ask about how much one drank: "When you drink, how much do you usually drink during a day's time? _____"

This procedure yielded a quantitative rather than a categorical measure of alcohol intake. The amount of alcohol consumed was recorded (e.g., a fifth a day) and converted to liquid ounces (e.g., $1/5 = 026$ ozs.) corresponding to the amount reported. The conversion scheme followed the procedure established in the National Treatment Outcome Prospective Study (cf., Hubbard et al., 1989). This method permitted alcohol consumption to be described as a continuous variable that accounted for individual variations in drinking.

The advantage of using the above procedure is that the values obtained relating to drinking behavior could be empirically defined as representative of problem drinking (e.g., the higher the alcohol intake, the more likely there may be alcoholic drinking).

A. THE ISI SAMPLE:
COMPARISONS WITH UNDUPLICATED SOC DATA

The group from which the ISIs were obtained consisted of 502 cases who used the SOC one or more times during 1989. This figure represented about a third of the total unduplicated entries.

It may be noted that a limitation of this part of the research is that it is based on a sample exclusively from the SOC, which means that it may have missed some homeless or other Skid Row inhabitants who did not use the shelter. This limitation, however, is not deemed to be restrictive because it is believed all of the regular Skid Row inhabitants used the shelter some time during the year, and because the primary focus of the study was to assess the characteristics of those who utilized the SOC. The characterization of this population provided a way of deriving an empirically based understanding of the characteristics of Anchorage's Skid Row, homeless or street population.

1. Characterizing the ISI Sample (Demographics)

Of the 502 cases comprising the ISI cohort, 83 percent were men and 17 percent were women. This compares well with the unduplicated count of 81 percent men and 19 percent women, which suggests that the ISI cohort was representative, by gender, of those who used the SOC in 1989.

The ethnic composition of the ISI sample, shown in Figure 40, closely approximated the distribution of the unduplicated sample. The age distribution of the ISI group, ranging from 18 to 72, with a mean age of 37.9 years, was also representative of the larger unduplicated group (mean = 37.1 years). Figure 41 shows a comparison of the two groups by age brackets. Inspection of these data indicate that the ISI group had a slightly higher representation of 35-44 year-olds than the unduplicated group.

Based on the comparisons described above the ISI sample was representative of the people who used the SOC during 1989.

2. Demographic Data Comparisons

(a) Comparison with a Previous Study of Anchorage's Skid Row Population

Kelso, Hobfoll, and Peterson (1978) undertook a descriptive analysis of the Skid Row population in Anchorage's downtown area. They interviewed 206 individuals, inquiring about demographic characteristics, background characteristics, family history, education and employment, drinking and drug-related behavior, housing and mobility, social service contacts, health and nutrition, and support systems. The current findings are compared to the find-

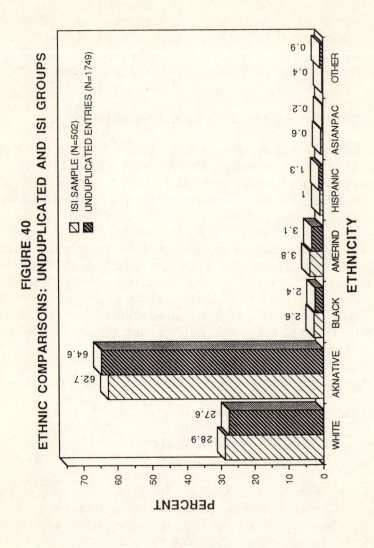

FIGURE 40
ETHNIC COMPARISONS: UNDUPLICATED AND ISI GROUPS

FIGURE 41
AGE COMPARISONS: UNDUPLICATED AND ISI GROUPS

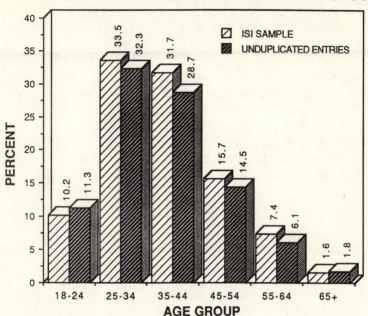

ings of the 1978 study in order to place them in perspective to observe changes over time. This comparison is presented in Table 3. The categories listed in the table are from the 1978 study to enable comparisons on similar variables. The additional data represents information obtained from the current study. In reviewing this data it needs to be stressed that it is possible that some of the same people queried in 1978 may have also been present in 1989, having been on the streets for at least 11 years.

Inspection of the data in Table 3 reveals that the ratio of males to females changed somewhat over time. Women currently represent 2 percent less of the street people compared to 1978, while men increased 4 percent compared to the previous findings. Males, however, predominate at a ratio of 5:1 in comparison to women.

The ages of the street people also fluctuated, generally reflecting an increase in older age groups. The 18-25 year-old group decreased since 1978, while 26-35 year-olds remained constant. Increases were noted for both of the two other age groups. The current group of street people thus tends to be older than recorded earlier, which may reflect (a) the continued presence of those on the street who were there years ago, or (b) an influx of generally older people. In either case there is a sufficient amount of young people congregating on the "Avenue" to have maintained a steady group of people within the 26-35 age range. The Avenue is thus constant and dynamic in that there is an established group of people who sustain themselves there and a group of younger people who are beginning to maintain themselves on the streets.

The ethnic composition of the street people showed several changes. Most apparent is that the proportion of Whites decreased (−10.6%) in comparison to 1978, while the Eskimo group in-

Table 3

Comparison of 1989 and 1978 Surveys of Anchorage's Street Population

	1989 (N=502)	1978[1] (N=206)
Gender		
Male	83.0	80.0
Female	17.0	19.0
Age		
18-25	11.2	19.7
26-35	36.3	36.7
36-45	27.9	23.4
45+	24.7	19.7
Ethnic Group[2]		
White	28.9	39.5
Eskimo	35.4	26.8
Indian	21.3	20.5
Aleut	9.0	10.0
Black	2.6	2.6
Asian	0.6	0.5
Hispanic	1.0	--
Other	1.2	--

	1989 (N=502)	1978 (N=206)
Marital Status		
Married	8.0	13.2
Divorced	26.1	28.4
Widowed	5.2	2.6
Separated	8.4	8.4
Not Married	50.7	47.4
Living as Married	1.6	--
Religious Denomination		
Catholic	15.6	19.1
Protestant[3]	16.7	16.3
Baptist	9.7	14.9
Russian Orthodox	14.2	9.9
Lutheran	3.7	9.9
Methodist	1.2	3.5
Other	7.3	26.2
Native American Church	18.1	--
Episcopalian	4.1	--
Mormon	1.6	--
Moravian	1.2	--
Presbyterian	1.6	--
Quaker	2.2	--
Educational Level		
3rd or less	1.4	1.6
4th thru 7th	7.0	8.5
8th grade	4.5	13.2
9th thru 11th	20.9	22.2
12th grade	53.4	37.6
past 12th	12.7	18.9
Veteran Status		
Veteran	31.2	44.2
Vietnam Veteran	11.6	--
Non-Veteran	68.8	55.8

[1] Derived from Kelso et al., 1978.

[2] Categories derived from Kelso et al., 1978.

[3] No denomination given other than Protestant

creased ($+8.5\%$). The Indian[1] group showed a slight increase (0.8%), while Aleuts decreased very slightly (-0.1%). The proportion of Blacks and Asians remained consistent.

The noticeable changes in the White and Eskimo subgroups reflects the effects of the economic condition in Alaska over the past few years. The decline in oil prices, beginning around 1985, led to a depressed economy resulting in many people leaving the state. This out-migration included transient and seasonal workers, largely white, who tended to "hangout" or live on the Avenue when not employed.

The Alaskan Native, in contrast to Whites, is less mobile in terms of leaving the state. Moreover, a depressed state economy brings people to Anchorage to look for jobs. Additionally, those hanging out in Anchorage are less likely to leave or go to other places in the state because there is no work in rural areas. Thus the large number of Alaskan Natives who tend to congregate in downtown Anchorage are there partly because of economic circumstances.

Fewer of the street people were married in 1989 than 1978, fewer were divorced, and more were widowed. There was also an increase in the proportion of those having never married.

There were varying degrees of representation from different religious denominations, with changes occurring in comparison to the 1978 data with respect to individual church membership.

Comparison of the educational level showed that the current group had a higher proportion of people completing the 12th grade, and fewer people with an 11th grade education or less. Fewer people in the current sample had an education beyond the 12th grade.

The current sample also consisted of fewer veterans than recorded in 1978, but of those who indicated they were veterans, 11.6 percent served in Vietnam.

Additional information describing the 1989 sample showed that of those married, the average length of time married was 9.6 years, with a range of 1 to 50 years. Fifty-three percent of the sample indicate that they had children, ranging from 1 to as many as 17.

The picture presented of the current street population is one of mostly men (8 out of every 10 persons), largely between 26 and 44 years of age, of which two out of ten are likely to be White, seven out of ten are likely to be Alaskan Natives, and one in ten either

American Indian, Black, Hispanic, Asian or from another ethnic group. Over half (50.7%) have never married or are divorced. A majority have completed a high school education. About one in three served in a branch of the armed forces, with just over one in ten veterans having been in Vietnam.

B. COMPARISON WITH OTHER
SKID ROW POPULATIONS

Table 4 presents a comparison of the Anchorage profile with data from a study of Los Angeles inner-city homeless people ("L.A. Study," Koegel & Burnam, 1987), and from a statewide study of homeless people in Ohio in both urban and rural settings ("Ohio study," Roth & Bean, 1985/86).

Most apparent among the three data sources is the consistently higher ratio of men to women. The age comparison with the L.A. sample shows that the Anchorage sample contained more people in the 31-50 age group and fewer older people. These same findings prevail when a comparison is made with the Ohio sample.

The findings are consistent with respect to marital status; separated/divorced or single people predominate. Education levels were comparable when compared to the L.A. sample. Veteran status was also comparable across the three groups.

The ethnicity data conveys an interesting difference that reflects on homelessness. In Los Angeles, for example, the predominate ethnic group among the homeless was Black (44.0%). In Anchorage the largest homeless group was Native Americans (67.5%). In contrast, Hispanics constituted 14.6 percent of the L.A. sample, while representing only 1.0% of the Anchorage group. Whites are about evenly represented in both samples.

These findings suggest that there are differences in the ethnic composition and social impacts on ethnic groups in different urban geographical locations. The LA data represents the ethnic composition of the region. An inner city survey, such as that conducted in LA, would identify Blacks as the most prevalent ethnic group because inner city inhabitants have, until recently, been primarily poor and unemployed Blacks. Conversely, the ethnic group most likely to be displaced in Alaska, specifically in Anchorage, are

Table 4

Demographic Comparison with Skid Row Studies

	Anchorage (n = 502)	Los Angeles[1] (n=317)	Ohio[2] (n=979)
Gender[3]			
Male	83.0	95.0	81.0
Female	17.0	5.0	19.0
Age			
<20	2.4	2.8	
21-30	24.8	30.7	
31-40	37.2	30.7	
41-50	21.4	15.5	
51-60	12.0	14.9	
61-70	2.2	5.4	
18-29	23.7		34.7
30-39	37.8		27.6
40-49	22.5		16.8
50-59	12.7		13.3
60+	3.2		6.4

Marital Status			
Married	8.0	2.5	9.0
Widowed	5.2	5.4	4.4
Separated/Divorced	34.5	33.1	39.0
Never Married	50.7	59.0	44.7
Living as Married	1.6	--	2.1
Ethnicity			
Black	2.6	44.0	--
White	28.9	30.7	--
Hispanic	1.0	14.6	--
Native American	67.5	5.7	--
Other	1.0	5.1	--
Veteran Status			
No	68.8	62.5	67.9
Yes	31.2	37.5	31.7
Viet Nam Veteran	11.6	--	8.5
Education (In years)			
Mean	11.1	11.3	--

[1]Ropers & Boyer, 1987.
[2]Roth and Bean, 1985/1986.
[3]Categories are derived from the LA or Ohio Studies.

Alaskan Natives. Alaskan Natives would thus tend to constitute the highest proportion of the homeless or street population in Alaska's largest city.

The findings about Blacks in Los Angeles and Alaskan Natives in Anchorage have an interesting implication. It clearly suggests that homelessness, or those who constitute a "Skid Row" population, represent an "ethnic specificity." That is, the constituents of any group of street people, such as Skid Row inhabitants, or other such type of group, represent the social-geographical composition of the larger society in which the people function. A Skid Row is thus a micro-society representing people who have been impacted to varying degrees by psychological, social, economic, and political factors. After reviewing the development of Skid Row districts in Philadelphia and Detroit, Blumberg et al. (1978), concluded that ". . . there are important differences with respect to the racial composition of the populations and the relationship of the two areas to the CBD [central business district]" (p. 70). Therefore the emergence of any dominate ethnic Skid Row group, and the composition of any related or associated ethnic groups, is not independent of the population characteristics that exist locally and the sociological/cultural biases maintained by the dominant population.

Blumberg et al. (1978) stated:

> We do find, in fact, Black Skid Rows in Black ghetto areas; we find small satellite White Skid Rows in White slum areas. In both cases the Skid Row-like residents blend in with others who are less Skid Row-like. The residents of the central skid Row are not like others who live nearby, who are usually upper-middle class. The Black Skid Rows are maintained by the segregation of American society, the satellite White Skid Rows by some remaining ties to 'neighborhood.' (p. 190)

Nevertheless, once a generally unique "Skid Row" is constituted, the behavior that takes place within it becomes similar to other Skid Rows more than just in terms of form. The consequences are the same, as are the standards of behavior that develop within the group regarding drinking practices and ways to deal with homelessness and poverty.

1. Homelessness

The definition of homeless established for this study — those reporting no permanent address or place to stay other than a shelter or the streets — is generally consistent with criteria specified in other research. Gelberg et al. (1988), for example, defined a homeless person as one who spent the preceding night in (1) an emergency shelter, (2) outdoors, (3) any space not designed for shelter, (4) a hotel, motel, or home of a relative or friend and was uncertain whether he or she could continue to stay there, and (5) stated that he or she did not have a permanent house or apartment to which he or she could go.

Based on these criteria, 99.7 percent of the ISI cohort were homeless. This figure coincides with a finding of 99.9 percent homeless among Los Angeles inner city or Skid Row people reported by Koegel and Burnam (1987).

When attempting to evaluate the extent of homelessness more precisely among the ISI sample, 31.7 percent reported they had a regular place to stay, thereby reducing the proportion of homeless to 68.3 percent of the sample when this data is taken into account. "Regular," however is considered by the street people to be the Brother Francis Shelter (BFS), and they give the shelter as their permanent address. For example, when asked where one usually sleeps, 65.4 percent indicated BFS. Only 0.3 percent stated they slept in a permanent type of residence (e.g., with a spouse). Further inquiry of where people slept the night before resulted in only 0.9 percent having spent the night with family. The remainder slept either at a shelter (BFS, 30.7%; SOC, 52.8%) the street (6.5%), with friends (4.1%), or other places (5.0%). Ropers and Boyer (1987) found that 49.4 percent of their sample stayed in a shelter the previous night, and that 28.3 percent spent the night on the street.

Table 5 lists where respondents reported having spent the past few weeks prior to being interviewed, and the places at which they said they spent the most time.

The data shows that 10.3 percent used their house or apartment to sleep in the recent past. Some (17%) used a friend's place, while almost a third (29.9%) stayed on the street. Ten percent were in jail or prison, some were in a hospital or institution (7.9%), while oth-

Table 5
Living Arrangements

**Other Places Reported Sleeping by SOC Clientele
For a Few Prior Weeks**

	Percent
Own house or apartment	10.3
A rooming house	5.8
A hotel or motel	21.4
A friend's place	37.4
A relative's place	19.6
A halfway house	6.4
In a jail or prison	10.8
A hospital or institution	7.9
Detox	8.2
The street	29.9
A car, truck or van	7.9

Place Reported having Stayed Most Frequently

	Percent
Street	9.9
Friends	17.0
Spouse	0.3
Family	5.6
Sleep Off Center	4.3
Brother Francis Shelter	46.0
Camp	2.8
Own residence	2.8
Car, truck or van	1.9
Rooming house	.9
Hotel/Motel	2.2
Halfway house	2.8
Jail	0.6
Hospital or Institution	0.3
Other	2.8

ers were in a detox program (8.2%). The place that was reported most frequently was the Brother Francis Shelter (BFS).

The data in Table 5 reflects the transient nature of the homeless, with their staying/sleeping at different places. Kelso et al. (1978) also found a high degree of mobility among the Skid Row population in their study.

The transient nature of this population was also reflected in the finding that only a quarter of the sample (25.9%) considered Anchorage their hometown; 64.8 percent said that they came from someplace else in Alaska, 3.7 percent were from out of state and 5.6 percent were from outside the U.S.

2. Employment Status

Eighty-four percent of the ISI cohort indicated that they were not currently working, as shown in Table 6. Among 307 cases that reported having worked at some time in their life, 62.6 percent worked within the past year, while 36.2 percent were employed more than a year ago. Table 6 lists the type of work reported by ISI respondents.

The largest number of respondents worked as unskilled laborers

Table 6

Occupations Reported by ISI Respondents

LAST TYPE OF JOB

Occupation	Percent[1]
Professional/Technical	2.2
Business/Sales	2.7
Skilled Labor/Fishing	33.7
Unskilled labor	55.0
Clerical	1.5
Other	3.2
No skills	.7

[1](N=407)

(55%), while a third (33.7%) worked as skilled laborers or fishermen. These two job classifications are primarily representative of the seasonal nature of employment in Alaska.

Comparisons of some of the current findings pertaining to homelessness, employment, and other variables with those from The Anchorage Skid Row study by Kelso et al. (1978) are not possible because Kelso et al. did not report such data. Instead, they divided their sample into three subsamples: (a) Agency People, those who used public services and who were interviewed at a health or social service agency, (b) Street People, who were interviewed on the street and who did not utilize any public agency, and (c) Residential People, which consisted of people with a residence but who tended to stay on the streets. Kelso et al. evaluated their data on the basis of differences among these three groups, and how they impacted the social service system. Their research was largely a social impact study and not ethnographic research. The procedures followed in the present study did not pursue a comparable methodology.

C. DRINKING BEHAVIOR

Alcoholism has always been associated with a Skid Row population, and alcohol-related health problems have been historically found to be highly prevalent among Skid Row inhabitants. Drinking among Skid Row inhabitants has been attributed to such factors as shiftlessness and failure to obtain employment. Estimates of alcoholics among Skid Row populations range from over 80 percent (Straus, 1946), to 25 to 40 percent (Mulkern & Spence, 1984).

One of the major problems involved in studying homelessness and drinking is that of defining a causal relationship. Does, for example, drinking cause homelessness? Or does homelessness cause drinking? The answer is that neither is a direct cause of the other. There is clearly an interactive effect in which one variable sometimes weighs more heavily than the other as a causative influence, but this causal relationship is itself influenced to varying degrees by other factors such as availability of alcohol, money, peer influence, events in the community affecting the homeless, etc. To describe this complex relationship is difficult, at best, and precise knowledge may be elusive.

The following section describes the findings from an exploratory study of the drinking behavior of the study population, with special emphasis on attempting to discern relevant information about the relationship between drinking behavior and homelessness without inference to causality. Although the data will largely be confined to descriptive analysis, results from more detailed inferential analyses are reported when appropriate.

1. Daily Beverage Alcohol Consumption (in Ounces)

As discussed earlier, an assessment of alcohol consumption was made in terms of daily fluid ounces of beverage alcohol rather than the number of drinks, bottles, etc., consumed. Numerous reviews concerning the best method to assess drinking patterns and problems have been raised in the literature for decades (cf., Donovan & Marlatt, 1988; Room, 1977), with no one procedure emerging as the single best method. Nevertheless, the most widely used method to acquire information about drinking behavior is from self-reports from a target population. The reliability of self-reports, however, is an issue of concern (cf., Baekelan, Lundwall, & Kisen, 1975; Sanchez-Craig, & Wilkinson 1986/87). This problem takes on special significance when Skid Row inhabitants are being studied because the stereotype of the Skid Row alcoholic is one of dishonesty (Bahr, 1973).

Annis (1979), in attempting to determine the reliability of Skid-Row alcoholic's self-report on a number of variables, found relatively high response agreement on reinterview for demographic items, but less reliability for questions about social functioning and drinking patterns.

In order to attempt to control for potential unreliable responses, the procedure of inquiring about the person's alcohol consumption in terms of self-reports of an actual day's consumption permitted conversion to fluid ounces of beverage alcohol. The attainment of a statistical estimate of daily beverage alcohol consumption allowed calculation of the magnitude of any statistical errors, thus yielding a range of alcoholic beverage consumption which characterizes the given data set.

The daily alcoholic beverage consumption reported for 392 cases of the ISI ($N = 502$) subgroup is described in Figure 42. (Data for 110 cases, or 20%, were missing.) It should be noted that these data are based on responses to the following question: "When you drink, how much do you usually drink during a day's time?" The statistics derived from the analysis of the data represent a summation of the person's self-report of what was consumed, that is, either one type of beverage or a combination of alcoholic beverages. The preferences for alcoholic beverages were: 54.1 percent indicating that they drank whiskey; 1.5 percent wine; 29.7 percent beer; and 14.6 percent reporting that they drank all three types of beverages.

The results showed a wide distribution of consumption, ranging from a low of zero (7.7% of the ISI group) to over 301 ounces. Most respondents (34.9%) indicated drinking between 21-40 ounces daily, which corresponds to about 2.5 pints of whiskey. The mean consumption was 83.3 ozs. (SD = 08.4, SE = 5.47). When this average figure is converted into actual amounts of beverage

FIGURE 42
DAILY BEVERAGE ALCOHOL CONSUMPTION IN OUNCES

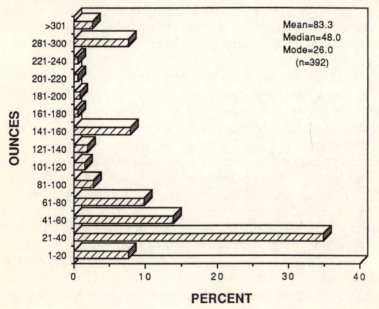

alcohol it approximates to over 7 (12-oz.) bottles of beer, or 5.2 pints of whiskey (or 3.2 fifths of whiskey), amounts which appear to be exceptionally high. Recent anecdotal reports from the SOC and the Alaskan Native Hospital of people with BALs of .60 and higher (one case was reported to have survived a BAL greater than .70), who were walking and talking, attests to the extremely high rate of drinking among members of the street population.

When the data were converted into an approximate measure of absolute alcohol consumed the amount ranged from 0 to 108 ounces, with a mean value of 10.4 ozs. (SD = 13.6, SE = .685). This conversion represents a very rough general estimate because it represented the combination of all three beverages; it did not calculate the values for beer, whiskey and wine separately because amounts consumed for each beverage were not obtained.

Despite the measurement/conversion problems, the finding from the Anchorage Skid Row sample clearly suggests heavy alcohol consumption by many respondents.

Although the derivation of the amount of alcohol consumed on a given occasion provides a good general picture of intoxication on that occasion, it does not convey whether it is an indicator of a person's everyday life, or a regularly recurring activity, or a special or infrequent event (Room, 1977). In order to provide a more representative measure of the individual's drinking behavior, the blood alcohol level attained for each person was used to typify drinking behavior. Few studies have characterized their data in these terms because such empirical data has been lacking. The values used in the following section represent the average blood alcohol level attained on entry to the SOC by each person during 1989.

2. Alcohol Consumption Measured by Blood Alcohol Level

(1) Average Blood Alcohol Levels

Figure 43 reports the average blood alcohol level (BAL) for 470 cases from the 502 members of the ISI cohort. The BAL groups used in this analysis of the data have been separated by an interval of 0.05, as opposed to 0.100 used previously. The smaller interval allowed a more detailed analysis of a fewer number of subjects.

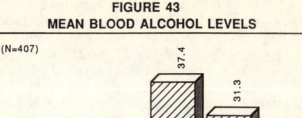

FIGURE 43
MEAN BLOOD ALCOHOL LEVELS

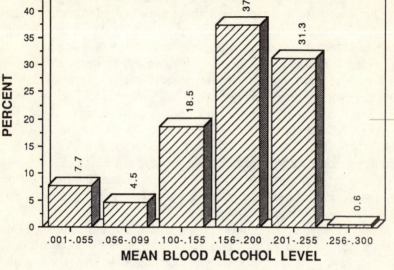

The average mean BAL was .168 (SD = .059). Scores ranged from a low of .001 to a high of .287.

Inspection of the data in Figure 43 reveals that the largest proportion of people (37.4%) attained an average BAL between .156 and .200, followed by 31 percent who achieved levels between .201 and .255. The distribution in Figure 43 is definitively skewed toward high BALs.

(2) Ethnicity and BAL

Figure 44 shows the relationship between ethnicity and average BAL during 1989. Given the few cases who were not White or Alaskan Natives, ethnicity, for statistical purposes, was categorized into three groups: White, Alaskan Natives, and Others (which included nonalaskan American Indians).

Observation of Figure 44 reveals a different trend for Alaskan

FIGURE 44
AVERAGE BLOOD ALCOHOL LEVEL AND ETHNICITY

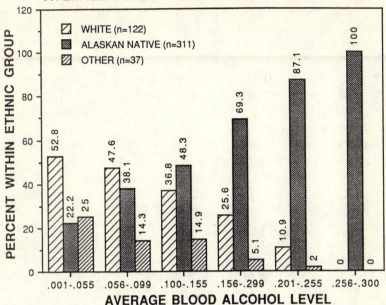

Natives than for Whites and Others. While the Alaskan Natives group showed a clear increase in the proportion of people drinking at higher BALs, the other two groups declined.

A statistically significant analysis of variance (ANOVA) was found between average BAL and ethnicity (F = 35.225, df = 2, $p < .001$). The mean average BAL for the White category was .137. It was .186 for the Alaskan Native group and .117 for the Other category. It can be concluded that there is a difference with respect to the way in which members of the three ethnic groups drank over the year.

A further evaluation of the BAL data disclosed that there was a not a statistically significant difference between gender and average BAL, and between age and average BAL. It thus appears that a major factor related to level of drinking in the sample is ethnicity.

(3) Length of Drinking

The relationship between length of drinking (in years) and the mean BAL level is presented in Figure 45. The data in Figure 45 represents the average BALs obtained from repeated measurement of the same individual during 1989. The mean drinking length was 20.5 years (SD = 10.1, SE = .493), and ranged from 1 to 55 years. The very small number of cases who drank for over 46 years, or who achieved a BAL greater than .255 (n = 5) were omitted from the data in Figure 45.

Inspection of the results show that as length of time increases variations occurred with respect to BALs. The number of years people in the sample were drinking ranged from less than five to over forty years. The general pattern indicates that those who drank at a low BAL (.001-.055), and moderately low levels (.056-.099), tended to stabilize their drinking over time, while those who drank at a higher level varied greatly with respect to their alcohol intake. The highest average BAL group (.201-.255) showed a steady increase in the proportion of people drinking at this level until 26-30 years, after which a decline occurs. In contrast, the percentage of people having drunk at a slightly lower level (.156-.200) tended to increase over a lengthy time interval. The same phenomenon is characteristic of those drinking within the .100-.125 BAL.

An ANOVA was applied to the data to determine if there was a significant difference between BAL groups with respect to length of years drinking. The results of the analysis revealed that the differences between the BAL groups, with respect to length of years drinking, was statistically significant (F = 2.635, df = 10, p < .01). This finding indicates that each of the BAL groups had a different drinking history (years drinking) with respect to their current level of alcohol consumption.

Further statistical analysis of the variable "length of drinking" found no significant differences between it and gender and ethnicity, which was grouped into three categories based on ethnic distribution in the sample (White, Alaskan Natives and Others). It thus appears, despite the disproportionate ratio of males to females (almost 5:1), and the large Alaskan Native representation in the sample (62.7%), that the drinking behavior, represented by the average

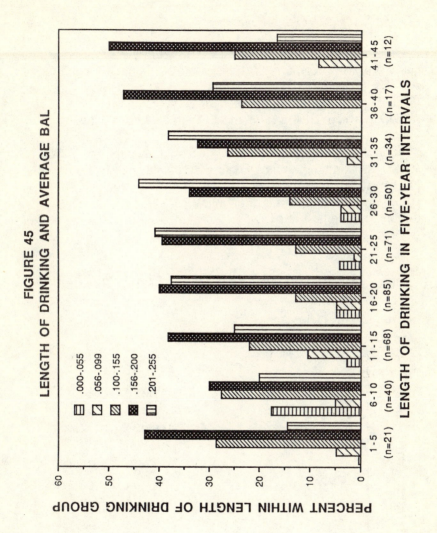

FIGURE 45

LENGTH OF DRINKING AND AVERAGE BAL

BAL during 1989, is consistent across gender and ethnicity in the ISI sample.

(4) Age Started Drinking Regularly

One of the questions asked was: "How old were you when you started to drink regularly?" The mean age obtained for 405 cases was 18.02 years (SD = 4.8, SE = .231). Almost 78 percent (77.6%) started drinking between 10-20 years of age, 20.5 percent started between 21-30 years, and 1.9 percent began between 31-40 years.

Figure 46 shows the relationship between average BAL and age started drinking regularly. These data display reasonably similar patterns for each of the three age started groups. What is of interest is that the people drinking the longest (31-40 yrs.) tended to have drunk at the highest level, while those drinking the least number of

FIGURE 46
AVERAGE BAL AND AGE STARTED DRINKING REGULARLY

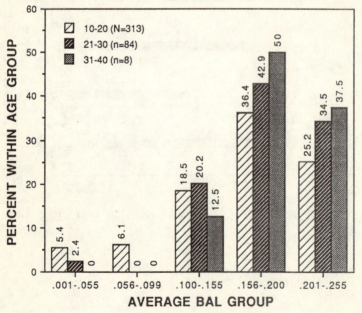

years (10-20) showed the lowest proportion of people drinking at the higher BALs. The Chi Square value obtained for the relationship between average BAL and age started drinking regularly was not statistically significant, indicating that average BAL and length of drinking are independent of each other.

Further statistical analysis of the data revealed that there was a significant difference ($F = 16.1$, df $= 1$, $p < .001$) between males and females concerning their reports of when they started drinking regularly. The mean age for males was 17.6 years (SD $= 4.4$), and 20.1 years (SD $= 6.0$) for females. Males began to drink regularly at earlier ages than females. No significant differences were obtained between age started drinking regularly and ethnicity. Thus while there may be gender differences related to initiation to regular drinking, members of the different ethnic groups all appeared to have started their "regular" drinking around the same time which, on the average, is during the late teen years for men and during the early post-teen years for women.

The age of onset of drinking has been found to be an important factor related to alcoholic deterioration (Lee & DiClemente, 1985). The importance of this variable is that "steady and excessive alcohol intake at an early age has more serious effects on the social, interpersonal, and physical and cognitive areas of an alcoholic's life than does the duration of excessive intake" (Lee & DiClemente, 1985, p. 400).

(5) Binge Time

Another question asked on the ISI was "How long have you been on this binge?" Binge time was defined as the period of time representing their current drinking episode, that is, since the last time they were sober for a day or more. The mean was 23.8 binge days (SD $= 33$), with a range of 1 to 91 days. The relationship between average BAL and binge time is presented in Figure 47.

These data, when it is grouped into two intervals representing the number of days on a drinking binge (1-30 and 31 +), show two very similar patterns. The Chi Square value obtained for this data was not statistically significant, indicating that the two variables are independent of each other. Additionally, there were no significant

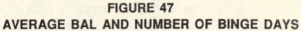

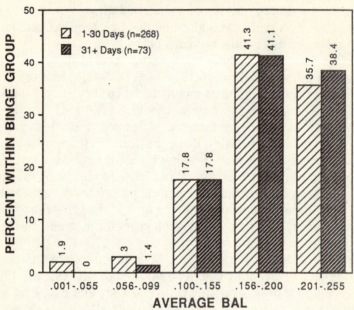

FIGURE 47
AVERAGE BAL AND NUMBER OF BINGE DAYS

differences between binge time and ethnicity and binge time and gender.

In summary of the findings related to drinking behavior, the homeless population, represented by the ISI sample, identified itself as a heavy and steady drinking population. The predominance of Alaskan Natives among the homeless or Skid Row population is reflected in higher rates of alcohol consumption in this group, which is consistent across gender. Generally, men started drinking earlier than women, and one's current drinking behavior was found to be related to length of drinking, regardless of ethnicity or gender.

D. BAL, INTOXICATION AND ALCOHOLISM

With the above findings in mind, the discussion turns to the issue of the relationship between BAL and intoxication and BAL and alcoholism. Thus far this problem was deferred because relatively large numbers of duplicated data were presented with an emphasis on descriptive analysis. The ISI cohort, however, presented a study group with which to explore more precisely the implications of the BAL data.

An important concern in interpreting the BAL data is establishing cut-off points to represent different stages or levels of intoxication. The determination of intoxication is influenced by many factors in addition to the alcohol consumption itself, e.g., body weight, gender, tolerance, food in the stomach, type of beverage consumed, etc. The BAL, however, provides a relatively good indication of alcohol misuse (Teplin, Abram, & Michaels, 1989). Given that the sample group's BAL has been averaged over the number of times each person entered the SOC during 1998, the data should reflect the extent of problem-related drinking. Nevertheless, it is critical to note that an attempt was made to distinguish between excessive drinkers among homeless men and women and not between homeless people who drink excessively and those who do not. As Straus and McCarthy (1951) noted, not all homeless people who drink may have a condition diagnosable as alcohol addiction.

Although the use of the BAL provides an empirical base to infer intoxication, no precedence for using BALs to categorize subjects has been established. Teplin et al. (1989) selected cutoff points based on the criteria for legal intoxication (above and below BAL = 0.100). The range of BALs obtained in the present study, together with the BAL intervals used to categorize the data, require more definitive criteria. As Clark (1966) has noted, "There is value in . . . identifying the heavier drinkers in the population regardless of what arbitrary limit is used to divide the sheep from the goats. It is not necessary to settle conclusively on what is excessive in order to explore association between heavy drinking and various social and physical ills" (p. 649).

In the present study cutoff points were chosen at different levels in the distribution of BAL data to obtain a differentiation between varying conditions of intoxication. The criteria selected for categorizing subjects, derived from Ray and Ksir (1990) and Segal (1988), is based on the relationship between blood alcohol level and alcohol's depressant effects on the central nervous system. (See Appendix 1.) These criteria are: *Unintoxicated* (.001-.050), *Intoxicated*

(.045-.155), *Moderately Intoxicated* (.156-.200), and *High Intoxicated* (.201 +).

The following is an analysis of the ISI cohort, focusing on identifying variables that may discriminate among drinking levels based on the average BAL data. The classification scheme differs from the BAL categories used previously in this report in that the earlier levels represented intervals not based on different stages of intoxication. The intervals used here are more representative of differences in levels of intoxication based on the behavioral effects of alcohol.

Drinking Levels

Figure 48 shows the distribution of average BALs by the classification scheme for the sample by gender. Totally, over a fifth of the sample (23%) drank at an intoxicated level, over a third (37.4%) drank at a moderately intoxicated level, and nearly a third (31.9%) drank at a highly intoxicated level. The average BAL was 0.156. The maintenance of this level or greater over a year's time can be considered to reflect problem-related drinking, and most likely represents alcoholic drinking. This finding suggests that a large segment of the homeless population (69.3%) were drinking alcoholically.

When the data are examined by gender, as shown in Figure 48, it is evident that while men outnumbered women (by more than a 5:1 ratio), women also drank heavily. Surprisingly, the women showed a higher average BAL (mean BAL = .182) over the year than men (mean BAL = .165), but this difference was not statistically significant. What the findings reveal is that both men and women drank at remarkably high levels, with more men drinking than women. This finding is consistent with Wright et al. (1987) who found that the general pattern of problem drinking was more common among homeless men than among women. The findings suggest further, however, that women, while less numerous than men among homeless subpopulations, tended to drink more, on the average, than their male counterparts.

Given the high rate of problem drinking assumed to occur within the sample, many of the Skid Row inhabitants can be considered to

FIGURE 48
BEHAVIORAL EFFECTS OF DRINKING BY GENDER

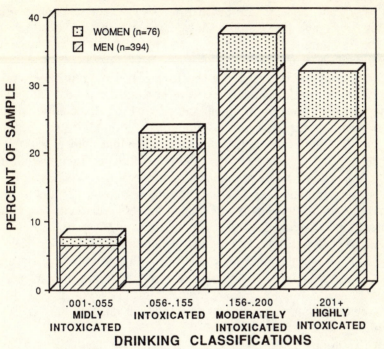

be at a high risk for or to be experiencing health and social problems (U.S. Depart., 1990).

The estimated level of problem-related or alcoholic drinking greatly exceeded prevalence estimates of 11 to 15 percent for men and 2 to 4 percent for women within the general population (Homeless, 1988). The findings also exceed the rate of alcoholism reported in other studies, which estimated that approximately 25 to 40 percent of homeless men suffer from serious alcohol problems (Homeless, 1988). The level of alcoholic drinking among the Anchorage Skid Row population also surpassed the findings from four major Skid Row surveys that found that between 33 and 40 percent of the Skid Row residents drank to excess (Bahr, 1969).

The results for men were generally consistent with Straus' (1946) finding that 80 percent of the homeless men in his study could be considered alcoholics. The findings, however, surpassed the levels of alcoholic drinking reported by Bahr (1969) from other studies: Bowery men, 36%; Camp LaGuardia, 47%; Chicago-Minneapolis study, 38%; and Philadelphia study, 26%. No data has been found in the literature which cites the occurrence of drinking among Skid Row women.

Following the derivation of the four criterion groups, separate stepwise discriminant analyses were computed for each drinking level. That is, four discriminant analyses were calculated in which there were four criterion groups: unintoxicated, intoxicated, moderately intoxicated and highly intoxicated. The independent variables in the analyses consisted of the following 10 items, each representing a quantitative score or coded as dummy variables: gender, highest grade completed, age started drinking regularly, number of admissions to the local publicly funded alcohol treatment program, parent alcohol-related death, ever tried a drug, ever in drug treatment, ever in jail, age, and number of admits to SOC.

The results of the analyses yielded only one variable that contributed to group separation — number of admits to SOC — but this variable failed to predict group membership at a level greater than chance expectancy, achieving an overall "hit rate" of only 20 percent.

This finding indicates that it was not possible to differentiate among the criterion groups in a statistically reliable manner on the basis of the independent variables used in the analysis. It thus appears that the individuals in the different criterion groups may not have been sufficiently disparate from each other to achieve group separation based on the variables entered into the analysis. This lack of a significant group separation implies that although members of a Skid Row population may be drinking differently, they nevertheless tend to be similar with respect to certain life events and share some comparable attributes. These similarities may result not only from drinking, but from living a Skid Row lifestyle, or a combination of drinking and being homeless.

The series of reports preceding this section described the relationship between drinking behavior and demographic data such as age, gender, ethnicity, etc. Further analyses using the reclassification of the average annual BAL into the four criterion groups paralleled prior findings. For example, a cross-tabulation of ethnicity (White, Alaskan Natives and Others) with the four criterion BAL levels, showed that more Alaskan Natives drank at higher levels than members of the other two groups, a finding consistent with previous results. A statistically significant Chi Square value (Chi Square = 86.126, df = 6, $p < .001$) indicated that there is a relationship between ethnicity and BAL level. Additionally, as noted above, there was not a significant difference between level of drinking and gender. These drinking criteria, however, will be used to examine the relationship between drinking behavior and variables related to family background and treatment, which are described in the following chapter.

In summary, the data reveals a remarkable consistency about drinking within the sample. Extraordinary high levels of drinking were found among Alaskan Native men and women, with women surpassing men at higher BALs. Both groups, however, appear to be drinking alcoholically. Although there are some variations within the sample, it seems that the homeless street population, except for ethnicity, may be a relatively homogeneous group with respect to their demographic composition, drinking history, and patterns of drinking.

Furthermore, in contrast to some early reports in the literature that homeless men on Skid Row may not be the stereotype of the heavy drinker (cf., Bahr & Langfur, 1967; Strauss, 1946; Straus, R., & McCarthy, R. G., 1951), the existent data is indicative of a heavy drinking Skid Row or homeless population. What may be the case is that Skid Row occupants and patterns of drinking within a Skid Row population have changed over time (cf., Garrett, 1989). Given these changes, some of the findings from earlier Skid Row studies, particularly those describing drinking behavior, may no longer serve as a basis for generalization about contemporary drinking subpopulations predominated by Native Americans.

Additionally, Skid Row behavior or lifestyles, as noted earlier, may be culture-specific in that they are an outcrop of the social-cultural environment in which they occur. Once a Skid Row group defines itself the drinking behavior within it may be more of a function of the group's constituents and sociocultural conditions than any other factor. As Straus (1984) has stated

Many people repeatedly drink what for them is too much alcohol — not because of an inner felt need to avoid the pains of withdrawal or respond to the psychological reinforcement of alcohol's mood modifying benefits, but simply because they feel the need to drink in a particular way in order to comply with the cultural norms that prevail or abide by the amenities and meet the expectations of their particular social world. (p. 134)

Strauss has called such drinking "social dependence," which he described as largely applying to young people and to the onset of problem drinking.

The concept of social dependence may also be applicable to members of a Skid Row population in that their drinking is not independent of the group's drinking values and perceived expectations. The drinkers may not perceive themselves drinking alcoholically, or if they do such drinking may be interpreted as being acceptable within their current environment. (A term which can be used to describe such drinking is "maintenance drinking.") Bahr and Langfur (1967) have noted that "Heavy drinkers who select a skid-row residence do so in part because they seek the presence of others with whom they can maintain both their drinking patterns and some minimal primary relations" (p. 472).

The primary difficulty, however, is that while a social need may be met, the upkeep of excessive drinking, even in the self-perceived form of maintenance drinking, particularly over a long period of time, results in a complex interaction of alcohol-related health, social and psychological problems. Thus while social factors may have an important role in sustaining drinking among a Skid Row population, there is a need to develop an understanding of the relationship between social and psychological motives for drinking and the onset of alcoholic drinking and alcohol-related health and other problems. Additionally, the degree to which genetic factors determine an individual's varied response to alcohol also needs to be understood, as well as the nature of the interaction between biological and behavioral events.

E. DRINKING AND TREATMENT-RELATED BEHAVIORS

1. Entries to Detoxification and to Treatment

An inpatient medical detoxification program (3-5 days) was maintained by the Clitheroe Alcoholism Treatment Program until July 1, 1989. Given that a large percentage of ISI data was collected between January and June, 1989, the data is believed to be representative of the sample as of June 30, 1989. A total of 284 individuals (61.3%) entered Clitheroe's detox program. Fifty-seven percent had previously entered a detoxification program (including Clitheroe's) sometime during their drinking careers.

A total of 193 people entered the Clitheroe Alcoholism Treatment Program during their drinking careers, averaging 4.8 admissions per person (SD = 6.7, range = 1 to 46 times). Sixty-four percent of the sample had entered some type of alcohol treatment program (including Clitheroe). Of those having entered treatment, 51.2 percent indicated that they had completed a treatment program at least once.

Figure 49 shows the relationship between problem drinking classification and the number of entries into the Clitheroe program.

The data shows clearly that treatment admissions are constant across drinking levels. Aside from the largest proportion having entered treatment from 1-5 times, a few people drinking at the highly intoxicated level entered treatment 21 or more times. A smaller number of individuals who drank at a moderately intoxicated level entered treatment between 16-20 times.

2. Parents' Drinking

From 136 valid responses, 48.5 percent reported that the death of one of their parents was alcohol-related (mother = 20%, father = 28.4%); 81.8 percent (n = 413) of the sample reported that there was an alcohol-related problem in their family (relatives, spouse, siblings). Twenty percent reported that their father drank (n = 484), and 7.2 percent said that their mother drank; 34.3 percent noted that both parents drank, a finding which is lower than the 45 percent figure reported by Fischer and Breakey (1987) for parents' drinking among a homeless population in Baltimore.

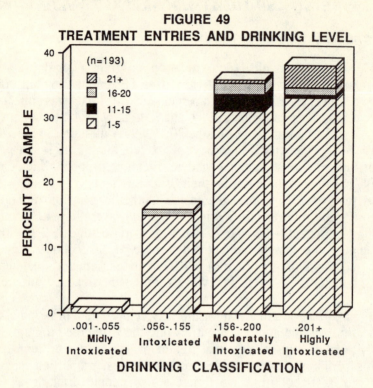

FIGURE 49
TREATMENT ENTRIES AND DRINKING LEVEL

Figure 50 shows the relationship between parents' drinking and BAL classification. The data in Figure 50 shows that drinking behavior appears to be independent of parental drinking or nondrinking in that distribution of drinking levels is fairly consistent across categories. The lack of a relationship between parental drinking and drinking level was supported by a nonsignificant Chi Square value of 10.79 (df = 9, $p > .05$).

An attempt to analyze the relationship between entry to treatment, represented by number of admissions to the Clitheroe Treatment Program and a set of independent variables yielded a very low, not statistically significant, multiple correlation of .19. The independent variables were: length of drinking, ever in jail, a parent's alcohol-related death, number of SOC admissions, race (White, Alaskan Native, Other), ever tried a drug, gender, age started drinking regularly, highest grade completed, veteran status,

FIGURE 50
PARENTAL DRINKING STATUS AND DRINKING LEVEL

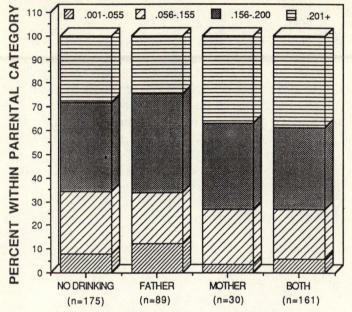

PARENTAL DRINKING STATUS

average BAL, ever entered detox, ever in a drug treatment program, and age.

Based on this finding it was not possible to derive a linear equation that described the relationship between number of entries to treatment and the set of independent variables.

F. DRUG-TAKING BEHAVIOR

1. Prevalence of Drug Use

In addition to drinking, 56.6 percent of the sample reported that they tried a psychoactive substance one or more times. Figure 51 indicates the proportion of the sample trying different chemical substances. The abbreviations in Figure 52 represent the substances listed below:

MJ   = Marijuana   HR = Heroin
HL   = Hallucinogens   TQ = Tranquilizers
LSD = Lysergic acid diethylamide IH = Inhalants
MR = Hallucinogenic mushrooms CK = Cocaine
PCP = Phencyclidine   ST = Stimulants
DP   = Depressants

As is shown in Figure 51, the substance tried by most of the sample (52.8%) was marijuana. Cocaine was next (32.7%), followed by hallucinogens (21.7%) and stimulants (20.7%). Of the specific hallucinogens tried, LSD showed the highest prevalence (17.5%). Heroin was tried by less than 10 percent (9.8%) of the sample, as were inhalants (9.8%). Depressants (13.7%) and tranquilizers (15.7%) had slightly higher prevalence levels.

2. Number of Drugs Tried

Figure 52 reports the number of drugs tried. Most (43.8%) did not try a substance, and relatively few (18.5%) tried only one substance, most likely marijuana. Cumulatively, 47.7 percent of the sample tried two or more substances.

3. Age and Drug Use

The relationship between age and experience with a drug is shown in Figure 53. Although the data do not reflect the recency of drug use it still permits an overview of the findings about age and drug use. As can be observed, as age increases experience with drugs decreases. Marijuana was the most prevalent substance used, followed by cocaine. The use of drugs does not appear to be restricted to a single age group, but ranges from 18-44 years.

4. Recency of Drug Use

Figure 54 shows the last reported time of use of a drug by those in the sample who indicated that they tried a substance. Inspection of these data show that the predominate time of use was greater than a year ago for all substances. Of those who used a drug recently, marijuana was used most, followed by cocaine. Both these substances appear to have been used during the past six months. Al-

FIGURE 51
LIFETIME EXPERIENCE WITH A DRUG

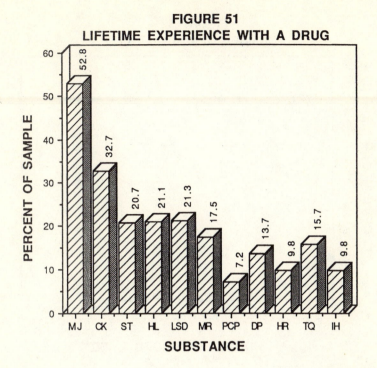

though other substances were used within the past six months, their use was lower than for marijuana and cocaine. A very small number of respondents used heroin during the past 24 hours and up to 3-6 days ago, suggesting possible active heroin use by a very limited number of street people (.8%).

5. Ethnicity and Drug Use

In contrast to drinking behavior, drug use was not a phenomenon primarily characteristic of Alaskan Natives. More Whites (73.8%) than Alaskan Natives (48.4%) tried a drug, as did members of the "Other" (66.7%) category.

FIGURE 52
NUMBER OF DRUGS TRIED

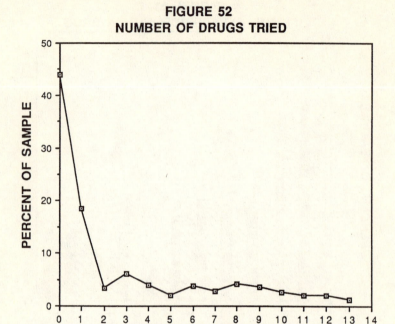

6. Gender and Drug Use

More males (60.3%) than females (42.7%) tried a drug, a finding which is consistent with the literature (Segal, 1990). A statistically significant Chi Square value of 8.67 (df = 1, p < .01), for the contingency table of ever tried a drug by gender, indicates that there is a relationship between gender and drug use.

7. Drug Treatment

The sample contained 60 people (12.2%) who reported that they had entered a drug treatment program (separate from alcohol treatment) at least once during their lifetime. Of these 25 (41.7%) indicated that they had completed a treatment program at least one time.

In summary, drug use was evident among the sample, particularly among those between 18 and 44 years. Over half the respon-

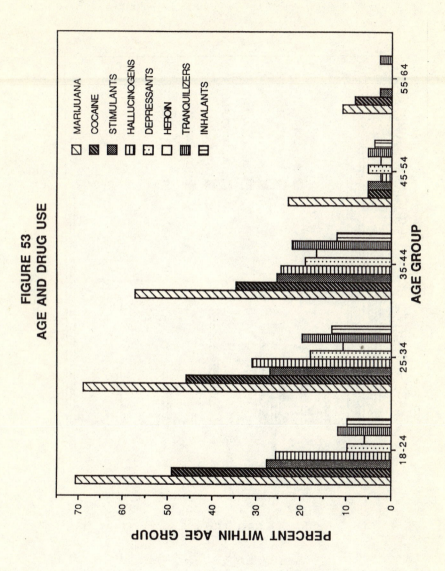

FIGURE 53
AGE AND DRUG USE

105

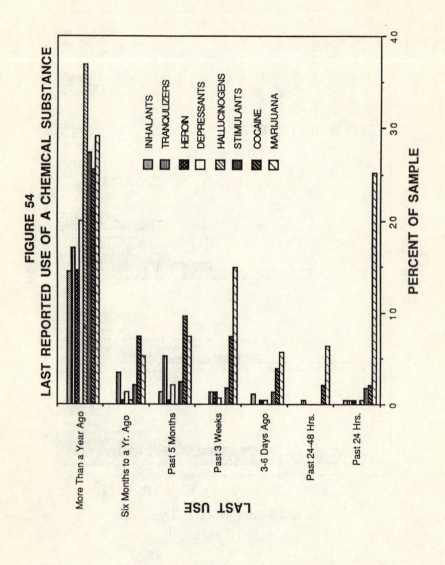

FIGURE 54

LAST REPORTED USE OF A CHEMICAL SUBSTANCE

INHALANTS
TRANQUILIZERS
HEROIN
DEPRESSANTS
HALLUCINOGENS
STIMULANTS
COCAINE
MARIJUANA

More Than a Year Ago

Six Months to a Yr. Ago

Past 5 Months

Past 3 Weeks

3-6 Days Ago

Past 24-48 Hrs.

Past 24 Hrs.

LAST USE

PERCENT OF SAMPLE

0   10   20   30   40

dents, of which two-third were men, tried one or more substances, some within the past 24 hours of having been surveyed. Marijuana and cocaine were most prevalent. A few (12.2%) were in treatment for a drug-related problem sometime in their life. More Whites tended to use drugs than Alaskan Natives or members of other ethnic groups.

As Garrett (1989) has noted, "One of the major differences between the 'new' and the 'old' homeless, is in reported drug abuse" (p. 321). Given that drug use was particularly notable among the younger people on the street, this trend has begun to evidence itself among the street population.

Estimates of lifetime prevalence of drug use among the homeless have ranged from a low of 10-15 percent to as high as 55 percent (Garrett, 1989). Based on the number of people reported having tried a drug in the current sample, it is apparent that drug-taking behavior within the sample was higher than 50 percent. Drug-taking behavior among the homeless may be becoming more prominent than estimated previously.

G. LEGAL INVOLVEMENT AND HOSPITALIZATION

1. Incarceration and Probation

Over two-thirds of the sample (69%) spent time in jail during their lifetime, and nearly two-thirds (57.95%) were in jail during the past year. Just over ten percent (10.6%) were on probation at the time of sampling. The percentage of people having been to jail is larger than that found by Gelberg et al. (1988) in their study of homeless adults (59%), and by Roth and Bean (1985/86) in their Ohio study (58.5%).

2. Hospitalization

Just over 16 percent (16.7%) of the sample were hospitalized for a medical problem during the past month.

SUMMARY

The picture of the homeless population that has emerged is that of a largely male, relatively young (mostly between 26 and 35 years) predominately Alaskan Native group, who maintain a rather steady and high level of alcohol intake. The streets and the shelters are their domain. Drug use also tended to be high among the younger members of the population. As a whole, however, despite ethnic diversity, the group tended to be more homogeneous than heterogeneous.

Homelessness and Skid Row affiliation appear to be synonymous among the street people in Anchorage. Few, if any, have a permanent home or roots in the community other than attempting to survive on the streets. The term public inebriate characterizes many in the group, who seem to remain consistently intoxicated. The shelters offer them food and a respite from the streets, but these are apparently insufficient to alter drinking, which has apparently increased over a year's time.

The question of why such drinking occurs is one about which theories abound, but for which a specific answer remains elusive. To say that they drink because they are homeless or homeless causes drinking is tautological. Other causes need to be identified. Given the predicament of the homeless public inebriate, many who are drinking alcoholically, the problem may not be one of seeking cause but rather one of needing to seek solutions, regardless of cause. Cause needs to be known for prevention, but its utility for successful intervention and rehabilitation of the chronic public inebriate may not be essential.

Another aspect of Anchorage's homeless or Skid Row population is that it has changed over a period of time. Chiefly, it has grown with respect to the presence of Alaskan Natives and decreased with respect to Whites. Today's group tends to be somewhat better educated, and somewhat older than a group identified earlier.

The Anchorage homeless Skid Row population is both alike and different from other identified Skid Row populations. As noted earlier, the observed behavior is similar to other Skid Rows, as are the problems created by a concentrated group of homeless drinkers. But the Anchorage group tends to be a heavier drinking group than reported in other Skid Rows.

While it has been noted that the Skid Row social system of heavy drinking is based on a well ordered social system (Rubington, 1968), Anchorage's Skid Row seems to be lacking a structured social system to regulate its drinking. Instead, two patterns of drinking may prevail: (a) drinking to maintain certain levels of alcohol in the blood stream over the course of a day, or (b) drinking as much as one can as fast as possible to get drunk and to stay drunk. Either drinking motive has resulted in exceptionally high drinking levels. The question is not whether such drinking patterns exist, but whether the drinkers have divided themselves into two separate drinking groups and if there are behavioral characteristics representative of each group. Thus drinking patterns may dictate social behavior, rather than the other way around.

Blumberg, Shiply, and Brasky (1978) have noted that "'Skid row' as a human condition is found in populations all over the poorer sections of the metropolitan cities, but there is a heavier concentration in the Skid Row locality" (p. 151). Anchorage is Alaska's metropolitan city, and as such it houses a large percent of the state's poor and homeless, which makes Anchorage the repository of many of the state's serious social and health problems, particularly those that are alcohol-related. Any possible solution to the Skid Row problem will have to take this factor into account.

NOTE

1. Alaska Athabascan and American Indians were combined into a single category by Kelso et al. (1978).

Chapter 5

Intervention and Treatment
of the Homeless Alcoholic

Public inebriates, until the 1960's, were subject to arrest for public drunkenness because public intoxication was illegal throughout the United States. What treatment existed was "handled primarily through brief periods of incarceration in the 'drunk tank' of local jails. At that time a handful of programs were established to provide medical detoxification for impoverished alcoholics in nonhospital settings" (Sadd & Young, 1987, p. 48).

The passage of the Uniform Alcoholism and Intoxication Treatment Act in 1971 ("The Hughes Act"), changed how chronic public inebriates were treated. Under the auspices of the Act states were to assume responsibility to establish standards to govern programs involved in the treatment and rehabilitation of alcoholics. The Act also encouraged shifting the care of the public inebriate from the criminal justice system to the health care system.

The foremost result of this Act was the evolvement of a more humane approach to the treatment of chronic public inebriates, largely encompassing medical detoxification and short-term (less than 30-day) programs.

The Sleep-Off Center, operated by the Salvation Army's Clitheroe Alcoholism Treatment Program, besides providing shelter for the homeless public inebriate, also served as a setting that provided intervention services to interrupt the addiction cycle of homeless alcoholics. Clients were encouraged to enter treatment, usually via a 3-5 day detoxification program that helped to "dry them out" to facilitate their entry into treatment. What follows is an analysis of the data about intervention (detoxification) and treatment (inpatient/

111

residential) for individuals who used such services at the Clitheroe Alcoholism Treatment Program.

A. DETOXIFICATION

As part of an attempt to intercede in the street-life and problem-drinking among the skid row population, the Salvation Army Clitheroe Alcohol Treatment program (SACC—Salvation Army Comprehensive Center) initiated a publicly funded detoxification (detox) program 12 to 14 years ago at Point Woronzof. Based on records dating back to 1984, 7,536 clients were serviced up to the end of 1988 at the 20-bed unit, averaging a stay of three to five days. During this period an average of 1,256 cases a year were admitted, which corresponds to an average of 105 cases per month. It is estimated, based on Clitheroe data, that approximately 60 percent ($n = 4522$) of these cases entered treatment at least once. The number who completed treatment could not be derived, nor could the number of multiple entries to detox by each individual.

The detox program was considered an essential part of the continuum of treatment delivered by the Clitheroe program. Detoxification represented a time out for street people, a means for them to reevaluate their status, for active motivation counseling to be pursued by counselors, and for medical intervention for cases in need of treatment. Of those who used the Sleep-Off Center in 1989, 136 entered SACC's detox program one or more times up to June 30th. The detox data reported in this section, however, are based on self-reported detox experience obtained from the 502 people who constituted the ISI sample.

Of the 502 cases constituting the ISI sample, 58.4 percent ($n = 289$) indicated that they had entered a detox program in Anchorage or elsewhere one or more times in their lives. Fifty-five percent ($n = 228$) reported that they had entered SACC's detox program one or more times. Of these, 13.3 percent had entered SACC's detox program during 1989. Thirty-seven percent had accumulated entries to SACC detox dating back to 1968.

1. Demographics

Table 7 lists the sociodemographic characteristics of the 228 clients who self-reported that they had entered SACC's detoxification program one or more times.

As is observed in Table 7, the detox program served a clientele who were basically younger, male, Alaskan Natives. The mean age was 39.4 years (SD = 10.66), and ranged from 19 to 67 years.

2. Client Characteristics

Table 8 lists some client characteristics associated with detox admission.

Most cases entered detox between 1-5 times (80.6%), with few cases (4.1%) having entered 21 or more times. The general profile of those admitted to detox reflects a group who largely started

Table 7

Sociodemographic Characteristics of Clients Having Ever Entered SACC Detox
(n= 228)

Characteristic	Percent
Gender	
Male	86.4
Female	13.6
Age	
18-24	5.7
25-34	32.5
35-44	33.3
45-54	18.0
55-64	9.2
65+	1.3
Ethnicity	
White	23.7
Alaskan Native	71.9
Black	0.4
American Indian	3.9

Table 8
Detox Admission Characteristics
(N=228)

Characteristic	Percent
Drinking History	
Mother drink	6.8
Father drink	31.5
Both parents drink	40.1
Mother alcohol problem	4.2
Father alcohol problem	7.9
Mother and father problem	3.7
Ever tried a drug	54.9
Ever in drug Treatment	13.7
SACC detox entries	
1-5	80.6
6-10	8.7
11-15	3.1
16-20	3.6
21+	4.1
Age started drinking	
10-20 years	78.6
21-30 years	10.9
31-40 years	2.4
Problem drinking classification	
.001-.055	0.9
.056-.155	16.9
.156-.200	39.1
.201+	43.1
Length of drinking in years	
1-5	3.4
6-10	7.2
11-15	17.8
16-20	20.7
21-25	18.3
26-30	15.9
31-35	7.2
36-40	4.8
41-45	3.8
46-50	.5
51-55	.5

drinking during their teen years (78.6%), and who currently drink to where an average BAL level of .156 or greater was obtained (82.2%). (The mean age for when they started drinking was 17.9 years, and the average BAC was 0.188). Length of drinking varied from 1 to 55 years, with a mean of 21.74 years. Most detox admits drank between 16-20 years (20.7%). Over half the cases tried a psychoactive substance other than alcohol (54.9%), and 13.7% had entered a drug treatment program at least once.

Of those who entered detox, forty percent (40.1%) reported that both their parents drank, and 31.5% percent reported that their father drank. A few respondents noted that their father (7.9%) or mother (3.7%) had an alcohol problem.

3. Regression Analysis

A multiple regression analysis was conducted to attempt to predict detox entry (dependent variable was the number of entries to detox), on the basis of several predictor variables: ethnicity (Alaskan Native, White and Other), bingetime, educational grade completed, length of drinking, male or female, age, average BAL, and age started drinking regularly. Dichotomous variables such as gender and ethnicity were dummy coded for inclusion in the analysis. The results of the regression analysis yielded a multiple correlation coefficient of .20, which was not statistically significant. Based on this finding, entry into detox could not be predicted on the basis of the predictor (independent) variables.

In examining the partial correlation coefficients derived from the analysis, the only predictor variable that showed any degree of association with the dependent variable was average BAL ($r = .16$, $t = 2.47$, $p < .02$), but this correlation coefficient is too low to derive meaning.

Variables that intercorrelated are age started drinking regularly with males ($r = -.34$, $p < .001$), and age started drinking regularly with females ($r = +.34$, $p < .001$). The negative correlation for males suggests that being a male is associated with started drinking regularly at a young age (mean = 17.6 yrs.). The positive coefficient between women and age started drinking regularly indicated that being a woman is associated with drinking regularly at an older age (mean = 20.06 yrs.). Although these correlation coefficients are moderately low, the opposite direction suggests that there are aspects of drinking-related behaviors that differ between men and women. One of these differences is that men start drinking regularly at an earlier age than women. This difference, however, seems to be unrelated to subsequent use of a local publicly funded detoxification program.

Two other correlation coefficients obtained were between average BAL and Alaskan Native ($r = -.41, p < .001$), and average BAL and White ($r = +.41, p < .001$). These correlation coefficients indicate that higher BALs were associated with Alaskan Natives (mean BAL = 0.19; nonnative mean BAL = 0.12), and that Whites were associated with lower BALs (mean BAL = 0.12) than nonwhites (mean BAL = 0.19). These findings are consistent with earlier results, suggesting that there are differences in drinking patterns/levels across ethnic groups. These differences, however, are unrelated to use of a detox facility.

In summary, the detox program was used by the homeless drinking population, primarily by younger, heavy drinking, Alaskan Native males. No relationship was found between selected demographic and drinking-related variables and entry into Clitheroe's detoxification program.

B. TREATMENT

Treatment of the homeless or Skid Row alcoholic has been difficult, at best, and has presented an ongoing challenge to service providers (Frey & Miller, 1975). Part of the difficulty in treating the homeless involves having to deal with (a) the distrust of authority and disenchantment with service providers, (b) a transient population who fail to keep appointments and who turn up unexpectedly, (c) complicated cases that involve a multiplicity of needs, and (d) the obstacles provided by alcohol abuse and dependency on alcohol (Breakey, 1987). Homeless patients have been described as "the most severely and chronically ill that a therapist is likely to encounter. They are 'treatment resistant' and have minimal resources in material terms as well as in terms of their social environment" (Breakey, 1977, p. 45).

The Salvation Army maintains a publicly funded treatment program that provides a 28- and an extended 90-day residential program. Clients enter the program directly from detox or as walk-ins when detox is not necessary. A total of 65 cases, all of whom used the SOC one or more times, entered treatment after detoxification during 1989. The following data represents an analysis of these cases based on SOC and treatment-related data. ISI data was not available for all clients, and was therefore not included in this part of the research. The limited data, together with the few subjects, prohibited an extensive analysis of the data beyond an exploratory level.

1. Demographics

Table 9 provides a description of the demographic characteristics of those who entered inpatient treatment during 1989. All initiated treatment in the 28-day residential program.

Table 9
**Demographic Characteristics of Clients Entering Treatment
(N=65)**

Characteristic	Percent
Gender	
Male	91.0
Female	9.2
Age	
18-24	10.8
25-34	36.9
35-44	43.1
45-54	9.2
Ethnicity	
White	55.7
Alaskan Native	35.9
Black	4.7
American Indian	4.7

The treatment group reflects a cohort that is primarily White (55.7%), male (91%), and most likely between the ages of 35-44 (mean age was 34.12 years, SD = .292). Over a third of those entering treatment were Alaskan Natives (35.9%).

2. Treatment Admission Characteristics

Table 10 describes the client characteristics of those who entered treatment. Concerning the use of the SOC before and after treatment, most of the cases (72.3%) used the SOC less than 10 times before having entered treatment. The mean number of prior SOC admissions was 9.52 (SD = 14.7). After treatment there was an increase in the number of cases who used it 1-10 times, but a decline in the number of people using it 11-40 times. (Mean post-treatment SOC entries = 6.82, SD = 16.81.) The proportion of people who used the SOC 41 or more times remained the same after treatment. The difference between pre- and post-treatment is not statistically significant ($t = 1.33, p = .189$), however, suggesting that the changes between pre- and post-treatment entries to the SOC did not change as a function of treatment.

The total number of days in treatment, shown grouped in intervals of 9 in Table 10 ranged from 2 to 71, with a mean of 38.79 days (SD = 28.23). Based on a 28 day program stay for the primary treatment program, 50.8 percent completed the program, with a third of these cases referred to an aftercare program (either outpatient treatment or to a VA counselor). Half the treatment group indicated that they had been in treatment one or more times in other programs.

The BAL problem drinking classification in Figure 49 indicated that those seeking treatment tended to be heavy drinkers (mean BAL = .158, SD = .059).

3. Regression Analyses

Client characteristics at admission could influence the course and outcome of a particular treatment episode. In order to explore the relationship between selected client characteristics/attributes, two regression analyses were undertaken.

Table 10

Treatment Admission Characterisitcs
(N=65)

_____

Characteristic	Percent
Number of SOC admits before treatment	
1-10	72.3
11-20	12.2
21-30	6.0
31-40	3.0
41-50	1.5
50+	4.5
Number of SOC admits after treatment	
1-10	89.2
11-20	1.5
21-30	0.0
31-40	1.5
41-50	1.5
50+	4.5
Total number of days in treatment	
1-9	21.5
10-19	4.5
20-29	13.7
30-39	13.8
40-49	17.3
50+	19.5
Completed treatment	50.8
Aftercare referral	33.4
Problem drinking groups	
.001-.055	6.9
.056-.155	31.0
.156-.200	39.7
.200+	22.4
Ever in treatment	50.2

(a) Multiple Regression

The first was a multiple regression analysis in which the criterion variable, number of days in treatment, was regressed against five independent variables: Alaskan Natives, age, number of SOC admission before treatment, average BAL, and White. The resulting multiple correlation coefficient of .33, although suggestive of a linear relationship between number of days in treatment and the corresponding independent variables, was not statistically significant. Since this relationship could have occurred by chance, it could not be interpreted with any degree of confidence that the relationships established are meaningful.

Although the results of the multiple regression analysis did not demonstrate the extent to which the set of client characteristics were related to treatment, some intercorrelations were found. The correlation coefficient between having completed treatment and the number of days in treatment ($r = .48$, $p < .001$), indicates that the higher the number of days in treatment the better the outcome. This finding is self-explanatory.

A relationship between average BAL and Alaskan Native was also found ($r = -.52$, $p < .000$). This finding is consistent with that described above for those entering detox, in that higher BALs were associated with being an Alaskan Native. Also, as noted above, a relationship was found between being White and average BAL ($r = .34$, $p < .005$), indicating that lower BALs were associated with being White. A relationship was also noted between being an Alaskan Native and post-treatment SOC utilization ($r = -.34$, $p < .003$). This inverse relationship shows that higher post-treatment SOC use was associated with Alaskan Natives.

Post-treatment use of the SOC was also found to be related to average BAL ($r = .35$, $p < .004$). Thus the higher the average BAL, the greater the use of the SOC after treatment. It should be noted, however, that except for the first two correlation coefficients, the remaining are low and not supportive of a strong relationship.

(b) Discriminant Function Analysis

In order to try to further an understanding of which client characteristics are related to successful treatment, a second exploratory procedure, discriminant function analysis, was applied to the data. This technique attempted to determine which combination of variables best predicts membership in criterion groups. The criterion groups were successful ($n = 29$) and unsuccessful ($n = 29$) completion of treatment. The predictor variables were: age, number of pretreatment SOC entries, average BAL, White, and Alaskan Native. No statistically significant discriminating variables emerged.

There are four explanations for this lack of findings. The first is that the small sample size is insufficient to generate statistically significant results. A second is insufficient variance in the data to obtain meaningful results, which suggests that the population may be more homogeneous than heterogeneous on the dimensions measured in the study. The third is that the variables selected are not substantially interrelated. The fourth is that elements of the first three reasons interact to contribute to a lack of statistically significant and meaningful findings.

4. Treatment Outcome Evaluation

In order to pursue an assessment of treatment outcome, it was planned to compare a treatment and nontreatment group, specifically dividing these major categories into two sets of subgroups: Treatment members with positive vs. negative outcome, and a nontreatment group, which identified a subgroup who stopped drinking without any apparent intervention, and another group who continued to drink. The procedure, in essence, followed a controlled trial research design. In this context the general sample would have consisted of individuals who enter the SOC. Based on the characteristics of those entering treatment, a matched control group, comparable in size to the treatment group, could have been derived from among those who used the DSC but who never entered treatment. Comparisons would have been made among these groups at comparable time periods using similar questionnaires.

But the small number of successful ($n = 29$) and unsuccessful

(n = 29) cases precluded the development of sufficient statistical power to undertake a test for differences between those who experienced treatment and those who did not. These few cases, as noted above, may have contributed to the lack of findings of any of the inferential analyses undertaken. These analyses, it needs to be noted, were undertaken as exploratory procedures, and were not used to test hypotheses.

SUMMARY

The outcome of the chronic public inebriate in treatment has not been a success story. "One of the reasons for pessimism and stigmatization lies in the fact that many of the homeless are addicted to alcohol or other drugs" (Shipley, Shandler & Penn, 1989, p. 508). Additionally, as Shipley et al., state, "if the substance abuser does not wish to change or does not believe that change is possible, no treatment program, no matter how complete or excellent, is likely to yield positive results" (p. 508). Yet the treatment intervention showed a 50-50 split with respect to completing treatment, which is consistent with treatment outcome reports in the literature. Research, however, has been generally pessimistic about the potential for successful rehabilitation of the homeless alcoholic (Shipley et al., 1989).

Chapter 6

Conclusions and Recommendations

Homelessness and drinking appear to go hand-in-hand. Drinking seems to be the predominant factor that reinforces homelessness. When people become homeless and attached to alcohol, it then becomes extremely difficult to separate the drinker from alcohol.

The shelters in the compound (Brother Francis Shelter, The Sleep-Off Center and Bean's Cafe), aside from providing human care, appear to be doing nothing for the homeless except helping to perpetuate their existence. The community, in the form of assistance to the shelters, is only responding to an overwhelming need to get people off the street. There is little effort to help people achieve a new position in life. Few take advantage of treatment, and the outcome is problematical for those who do. Many use detoxification for time out from drinking, but soon return to the streets after discharge.

A general pessimism prevails about the potential for successful rehabilitation of homeless alcoholics (Shipley, Shandler, & Penn, 1989). The findings from this study do not provide any reason for optimism. The gloom surrounding the rehabilitation of the homeless alcoholic has been described by Breakey (1987) as being related to the experience of disaffiliation among the homeless. Furthermore, they don't trust institutions, are highly mobile, present a multiplicity of needs, and often suffer from mental disorders in conjunction with their drinking. They are not perceived by service providers as ideal clients, and because of all these circumstances they tend to be stigmatized and rejected from traditional health resources. (The question of whether the traditional health resources are responsive to the special needs of the homeless alcoholic needs to be raised. If the homeless person is unresponsive to a traditional

123

program, maybe it is because he/she perceives the program as anathema to their needs, and their lack of response is more a function of this perception than some of the factors described by Breakey.)

What is happening is that a cycle of drink and rest has been established, one that may emulate the "revolving door" game described by Rubington (1966). In this game the "drunkard" is the main character. The rules of the game are simple: The drunkards drink and the supporting cast — the police, the courts, service providers, and all others — help the players to play. Thus the main characters drink in public, either in a vertical or horizontal position, sometimes they assault another or others, or steal from a local store. The game proceeds in an orderly manner, everybody knowing their roles in whatever scenario arises. Despite any intervention such as arrest or detention, hospitalization, treatment, etc., the drinker is soon back on the street. The question that arises is how long will this game be played? It is too costly to prolong both in terms of human life and economic expense.

To a large degree the behavior shown by the homeless reflects the fact that they are part of a subculture that offers them few ways to escape from their predicament. Moreover, the drinking that takes place within this subculture may be the result of what its members believe their conduct should be, what they value and what they want. If a turnabout is to occur there have to be fundamental social changes in their lives. This change involves dealing with the source of the problem(s) that underlie or contribute to homelessness, and providing the individual with a viable alternative to subsisting on the street. Involved in this change is a need to help the individual gain a sense of *self-efficacy* — the feeling that one can control the outcomes in one's life that matter to them (Bandura, 1986). Peele (1989) stated that

> The only way to actually effect our addiction rates is to bring about basic change. While such change may be difficult, anything that fails to deal with the real source of the problem is wasted effort. The few therapies that are effective *succeed because* they work to change real social forces in people's environments. These forces include work opportunities, family

and community supports, and the moral and values atmosphere (and rewards and punishments) in people's lives. (p. 260)

A possible strategy to counter the problems created by the street population is to approach them from a joint health and social perspective. This strategy involves a coordinated effort that uses the system to impact individuals in a beneficial manner, rather than having individuals impact the system.

This tactic calls for the development of a case management approach, one that is gaining prominence in responding to the needs of the homeless mentally ill (Harris, & Bachrach, 1988a). In its broadest sense, case management involves coordination and management of a person's utilization of the system by coordinating and overseeing a person's overall treatment within the system. Its purpose is to establish an environment in which individuals are facilitated to remain in treatment and to use services after treatment is completed. "Case management not only provides a coordination of care but is actually a mode of therapy in itself and as such constitutes treatment independent of any other treatments with which the patient is involved" (Harris & Bergman, 1987, p. 296). The case management approach is a pro-active strategy rather than a reactive posture (Harris, & Bachrach, 1988b).

If any gains are to be made in decreasing the street population and its impact on the economy and health and social service agencies in Anchorage, emphasis should be placed on positive steps to help chronic individuals come to identify with stable, integrative, and problem solving perspectives to make a transition to independent functioning.

The nature of an intervention under the concept of a case management strategy can be strengthened by approaching the rehabilitation of the client in terms of the life options that are available to the public inebriate when deciding to continue to drink or not, that is, to break with the traditions of street living. This requires an evaluation of each case to decide the best intervention strategy. Figure 55 provides a general model that illustrates the decision process and proposed treatment strategies.

As can be observed in the model, once the client enters the

Figure 55
Intervention Scheme for the Public Inebriate

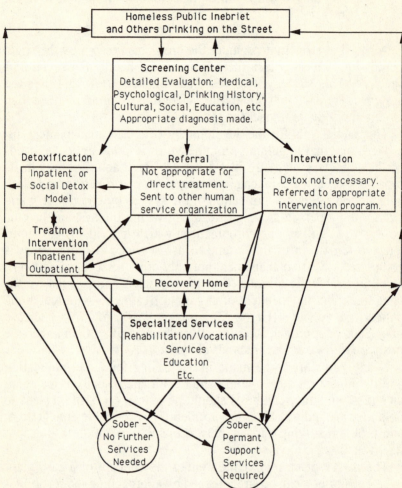

Screening Center, choice points occur about the rehabilitation of the client. Alternatives to treatment are possible, as are treatment options. The option selected is based on a thorough evaluation of the client along with the client's perception of which track to pursue. Emergency medical screening and medical referrals should be maintained on a 24-hour basis. The model resembles the intervention program established in Philadelphia to respond to its homeless problem (Shandler, & Shipley, 1987).

A treatment plan for each client should be worked out at the Screening Center (cf., Harris & Bachrach, 1988b) based on the evaluation obtained. After the development of the treatment plan, the individual should come under the guidance of a case manager who will become the client's advocate, and who will oversee the individual case to its termination. The strength of the case management model will rely, to a large extent, on helping chronic individuals identify with the stable and integrative aspect of the intervention program.

This conceptual scheme also provides for the evaluation and subsequent management of the dually diagnosed individual manifesting both a mental disorder and an alcohol- or drug-related problem.

The options available to clients after evaluation are referral to treatment, on an inpatient or outpatient basis, or to an appropriate agency for specific services.

A recovery home is introduced into the conceptual scheme. This place represents a residential center to serve as either a transitional or long-term facility that maintains clients after treatment, or to house individuals who do not require treatment. All clients residing in this facility would be eligible for specialized services to help establish or re-establish life skills necessary to function in the non-street world. Job-related training would be an essential component of such service. Based on the individual's needs and progress, a return to or establishment of a "productive" life-style would be accompanied by continued support and assistance, when necessary.

It should be noted that the above approach is not offered as a panacea. This statement is especially true because alcoholics, particularly street or homeless drinkers, have a way of "milking the system" so that it becomes a way of life. If not careful, shelters, service agencies, treatment programs, etc., while trying to respond to some of the basic needs of the chronic drinker, may also inadvertently contribute to sustain drinking behavior. The aim of an intervention program has to be on breaking the drinking cycle and helping to motivate clients to change. This is no easy task. "But people do 'make it' if they are involved with programs that can offer a range of resources, enough time for the client to gain the strength to move toward sobriety and goals that are realistic for both the client and the agency" (Shandler & Shipley, 1987, p. 56). The strategy that is outlined provides a basis to begin to conceptualize an intervention program to reverse the process of chronic homelessness and drinking.

There is, however, a caveat to this intervention model, which involves a need to incorporate an ethnically specific approach to treatment. This approach is especially relevant for Anchorage, where over two-thirds of the public inebriates are Alaskan Natives and American Indians. Culture specific treatment modalities have to be part of any treatment program that has ethnic-specific groups as its clientele. "Increasingly, evaluators, treatment personnel, and potential clients deplore the Anglo cultural bias of existing alcoholism intervention programs and call for integration of more traditional forms of healing practices into programs with large numbers of Native American clients" (Weibel-Orlando, 1987, p. 264).

Even in culture-specific programs, the aim has been to focus on the symptoms of alcoholism with little attention, if any, given to cultural factors and to cultural differences. Additionally, many ethnic groups, specifically American Indians and Alaskan Natives, experience difficulty in traditional programs because of a wide discrepancy between the client's world view and life experience and the treatment modalities in which they are required to participate, such as Alcoholics Anonymous. The lack of congruence between their value system and the one they are obligated to adopt creates a cultural conflict that contributes to an uncertainty about treatment and to relapse. Weibel-Orlando (1987), has found, for example, that all Indian treatment programs tend to show little affiliation with AA and turn instead to traditional healing approaches, which offers clients something with which they can identify.

The task, albeit a difficult one, and one for which there is no readily made solution, is to derive an intervention program that can deal effectively with cultural heterogeneity, one that addresses the specific needs of people from different ethnic backgrounds and different cultures (Weibel-Orlando, 1987). Treatment strategies need to be responsive to different cultural orientations and have to incorporate cultural experiences relevant to clients' cultural identities. Having counselors from different ethnic groups as well as using traditional cultural methods along with contemporary methods are part of the key ingredients that contribute to an ethnic-specific program.

Weibel-Orlando (1987) states that

> A first step toward reduction of high rates of recidivism among users of Indian [and other ethnic groups] alcoholism treatment programs may be to match treatment modality with client profile. [This profile could be obtained from] a central coordinating alcoholism treatment agency [that] determines the optimum fit of individual clients to treatment programs. Client placement would be based on the fit of client personality, sociocultural experience, spiritual beliefs, socioeconomic status, and level of acculturation to a program's treatment approach. In order for client-to-treatment fit to occur, lines of communication and transportation would have to be established and maintained between regional health services, mental health clinics, detoxification centers, Indian Health Service facilities, and all available alcohol treatment programs within a catchment region. (pp. 278-279)

The intervention program described above provides a framework for implementing Weibel-Orlando's treatment approach.

List of References

Anderson, N. (1923). *The hobo: The society of the homeless men*. Chicago: University of Chicago Press.

Andre, J. M. (1979). *American Indian Drinking Patterns*. Albuquerque, NM: Indian Health Service.

Annis, H. M. (1979). Self-report reliability of Skid-Row alcoholics. *British Journal of Psychiatry, 134*, 459-65.

Bahr, H. M. (1973). *Skid Row: An introduction to disaffiliation*. NY: Oxford University Press.

Baekeland, F., Lundwall, L., & Kissin, B. (1975). Methods for the treatment of chronic alcoholism: a critical appraisal. In R. J. Bibbins, Y. Israel, H. Kalant, R. E. Popham, W. Schmidt, & R. G. Smart (eds.), *Research advances in alcohol and drug problems. Vol 2* (pp. 247-327). Toronto: John Wiley and Sons.

Bahr, H. M. (1969). Lifetime affiliation patterns of early- and late-onset heavy drinkers on Skid Row. *Quarterly Journal of Alcohol Studies, 30* (645-656).

Bahr, H. M., & Langfur, S. J. (1967). Social attachment and drinking in Skid-Row life histories. *Social Problems*, 14, 464-472.

Bandura, A. (1986). *Social foundations of thought and action: A social cognitive theory*. Englewood Cliffs, NJ: Prentice-Hall.

Blumberg, L. U., Shipley, T. E., & Barsky, S. F. (1978). *Liquor and Poverty, Skid Row as a Human Condition*. New Brunswick, NJ: Rutgers Center of Alcohol Studies.

Blumberg, L. U., Shipley, T. E., & Moor, J. D. (1978). The skid row man and the skid row status community (with perspectives on their future). *Quarterly Journal of Studies on Alcohol, 32*, 909-941.

Breakey, W. R. (1987). Treating the homeless. *Alcohol Health and Research World, 11*(3), 42-46, 90.

Casement, M. R. (1987). The epidemiology of alcohol-related

problems among the homeless. *Alcohol Health and Research World*, *11*(3), 20.

Clark, W. (1966). Operational definitions of drinking: Problems and associated prevalence rates. *Quarterly Journal of Alcohol Studies*, *27*, 648-668.

Cook, H. F. (1910). *Report of the Social Secretary of the Municipal Lodging House for October 1910*. New York: New York Charity Organization Society.

Donovan, D. M., & Marlatt, A. G. (1988). *Assessment of addictive behaviors*. NY: The Guilford Press.

Fillmore, K. M. (1988). The 1980s dominant theory of alcohol problems—genetic predisposition to alcoholism: Where is it leading? In B. Segal (Ed.), *Alcoholism etiology and treatment: Issues for theory and practice* (pp. 69-87). NY: The Haworth Press, Inc.

Fischer, P. J., Breakey, W. R. (1987). Profile of the Baltimore homeless with alcohol problems. *Alcohol Health & Research World*, *11*(3), 36-37.

Frey, L. J., & Miller, J. (1975). Responding to Skid Row alcoholism: Self-defeating arrangements in an innovative treatment program. *Social Problems*, *22*, 675-687.

Garrett, G. R. (Fall, 1989). Alcohol problems and homelessness: History and research. *Contemporary Drug Problems*, 301, 332.

Gelberg, L., Linn, L. S., & Leaake, B. D. (1988). Mental health, alcohol and drug use, and criminal history among homeless adults. *American Journal of Psychiatry*, *145*(2), 191-196.

Goedde, W. H., Singh, S., Agarwal, D. P., Fritze, G., Stapel, K., & Pail, Y. K. (1989). Genotyping of mitochondrial aldehyde dehydrogenase in blood samples using allele-specific oligonucleotides: Comparison with phenotyping in hair roots. *Human Genetics*, *81*, 305-307.

Graves, T. D. (1971). Drinking and drunkenness among urban Indians. In J. O. Wadell & O. M. Watson (Eds.), *The American in urban society* (pp. 274-311). Boston: Little Brown & Co.

Graves, T. D. (1974). Urban Indian personality and 'culture of poverty.' *American Ethnologist*, *1*, 65-86.

Harris, M., & Bachrach, L. L. (1988a). *Clinical case management*. San Francisco: Jossey-Bass Inc., Publishers.

Harris, M., & Bachrach, L. L. (1988b). A treatment-planning grid for clinical case managers. In M. Harris, & L. L. Bachrach (Eds.), *Clinical case management*, (pp. 29-38). San Francisco: Jossey-Bass Inc., Publishers.

Harris, M. & Bergman, H. C. (1988). Differential treatment planning for young adult chronic patients. *Hospital and Community Psychiatry*, *38*, 638-643.

Harris, M. & Begman, H. C. (1987). Case management with the chronically mentally ill: A clinical perspective. *American Journal of Orthopsychiatry*, *57*(2), 296-322.

Heath, D. (1989). American Indians and alcohol: Epidemiological and Sociocultural Relevance. In D. Spiegler et al., (Eds.), *Alcohol use among U.S. ethnic minorities*, (pp. 207-222) (Research Monograph-18). Rockville, MD: NIAAA.

Hobfoll, S. E., Kelso, D., & Peterson, W. J. (1980). The Anchorage Skid Row. *Journal of Studies on Alcohol*, *41*(1), 94-99.

Hubbard, R. L., Marsden, M. E., Rachal, J. V., Harwood, H. J., Cavavaugh, E. R., & Ginzburg, H. M. (1989). *Drug abuse treatment. A national study of effectiveness*. Chapel Hill, NC: The University of North Carolina Press.

Institute of Medicine, (1988). *Homelessness, health, and human needs*. Washington, D.C.: National Academy Press.

Kelso, D., Hobfoll, S. E., & Peterson, W. J. (1978). *A descriptive analysis of the downtown Anchorage skid row population*. Anchorage, AK: The Center for Alcohol and Addiction Studies, University of Alaska, Anchorage.

Kogel, P., & Burnam, A. M. (1987). Traditional and nontraditional homeless alcoholics. *Alcohol Health & Research World*, *11*(3), 28-33.

Lee, G. P., & Di Climente, C. C. (1985). Age of onset versus duration of problem drinking on the Alcohol Use Inventory. *Journal of Studies on Alcohol*, 46(5), 398-399.

Lester, D. The heritability of alcoholism: Science and social policy. *Drugs and Society. A Journal of Contemporary Issues*, *3*(3/4), 29-68.

Lurie, N. O. (1971). The world's oldest on-going protest demonstration: North American Indian Drinking Practices. *Pacific Historical Review*, *40*(3), 311-332.

May, P. A. (1977). Explanations of Native American Drinking. *Plains Anthropology*, *22*(77), 223-232.

May, P. A. (1989). Alcohol abuse and alcoholism among American Indians: An overview. In T. D. Watts & R. Wright, Jr. (Eds.), *Alcoholism in minority populations* (pp. 95-119). Springfield, IL: Charles C Thomas.

McCook, J. J. (1893). A tramp census and its revelations. *Forum*, *15*, 753-766.

Mulkern, V., & Spence, R. (1984). *Preliminary results of homelessness needs assessment*. Boston: Human Research Institute for the Massachusetts Department of Mental Health.

National Institute on Alcohol Abuse and Alcoholism. (1987). *Alcohol and Health*. Rockville, MD: NIAAA.

Peele, S. (1989). *Diseasing of America: Addictions out of control*. Lexington, MA: Lexington Books.

Ray, O., & Ksir, C. (1990). *Drugs, Society, and Human Behavior (5th Ed.)*. St. Louis: Times Mirror/Mosby.

Reich, R., & Siegal, L. (1978). The emergence of the Bowery as a psychiatric dumping ground. *Psychiatric Quarterly*, *50*(3), 191-201.

Room, R. (1977). Measurement and distribution of drinking patterns and problems in general populations. In G. Edwards, M. M. Gross, M. Keller, J. Moser, & R. Room (Eds.) *Alcohol-related disabilities* (pp. 61-87). Geneva: World Health Organization.

Ropers, R. H., & Boyer, R. (1987). Homelessness as a health risk. *Alcohol Health & Research World*, *10*(2), 38-41.

Roth, D. & Bean, J. (1985/86). Alcohol problems and homelessness. *Alcohol Health & Research World*, *10*(2), 14-15.

Rubington, E. (1966). The "revolving door" game. *Crime and Delinquency*, *12*, 332-339.

Rubington, E. (1968). The bottle gang. *Quarterly Journal of Studies on Alcohol*, *29*, 943-955.

Sadd, S., & Young, D. W. (1987). Nonmedical treatment of indigent alcoholics: A review of recent research findings. *Alcohol Health & Research World*, *11*(3), 48-49.

Sanchez-Craig, M., & Wilkinson, A. D. (1986/87). Treating problem drinkers who are not severely dependent on alcohol. *Drugs & Society*, *1*(2), 39-67.

Segal, B. (1983). Alcohol and alcoholism in Alaska: Research in a multicultural and transitional society. *The International Journal of the Addictions*, *18*(3), 379-392.

Segal, B. (1988). *Drugs and behavior*. NY: Gardner Press.

Segal, B. (1990). *Drug-taking behavior among school-aged youth: The Alaska experience and comparisons with Lower-48 states*. NY: The Haworth Press, Inc.

Schuckit, M. A. (1987). Biological vulnerability to alcoholism. *Journal of Consulting and Clinical Psychology*, *55*(3), 301-309.

Shandler, I. W., & Shipley, T. E. (1987). New faces for an old problem: Philadelphia's response to homelessness. *Alcohol Health & Research World*, *11*(3), 54-57.

Shibuya, A., & Yoshida, A. (1989). Genotypes of alcohol-metabolizing enzymes in Japanese with alcohol liver disease: A string association of the usual Caucasian-type aldehyde dehydrogenase gene (ALDH) with the disease. *American Journal of Human Genetics*, *43*, 741-743.

Shipley, T. E., Shandler, I. W., & Penn, M. L. (Fall, 1989). Treatment and research with homeless alcoholics. *Contemporary Drug Problems*, 505-526.

Siegel, H. A., Peterson, D. M., & Chambers, C. D. (1975). The emerging skid row: Ethnological and social notes on a changing scene. *Journal of Drug Issues*, *5*, 160-166.

Singh, S., Fritze, G., Fang, B., Harada, S., Paik, Y. K., Eckey, R., Agarwal, D. P., & Goedde, W. H. (1989). Inheritance of mitochondrial aldehyde dehydrogenase: Genotyping in Chinese, Japanese and South Korean families reveals dominance of the mutant allele. *Human Genetics*, *83*, 119-121.

Solenberger, A. (1911). *One thousand homeless men*. New York: Russel Sage Foundation.

Stark, L. (1987). A century of alcohol and homelessness: Demographics and Stereotypes. *Alcohol Health and Research World*, *11*(3), 8-13.

Straus, R. (1946). Alcohol and the homeless man. *Quarterly Journal of Studies on Alcohol*, *7*(3), 360-404.

Straus, R. (1984). The need to drink "too much." *Journal of Drug Issues*, *14*, 125-136.

Straus, R., & McCarthy, R. G., (1951). Nonaddictive pathological drinking patterns among homeless men. *Quarterly Journal of Studies on Alcohol*, *12*(4), 601-611.

Teplin, L. A., Abram, K. M., & Michaels, S. K. (1989). Blood alcohol level among emergency room patients: A multivariate analysis. *Journal of Studies on Alcohol*, *50*(5), 441-447.

Teplin, L. A., Lutz, G. W. (1985). Measuring alcohol intoxication: The development, reliability and validity of an observational instrument. *Journal of Studies on Alcohol*, 46(6), 459-466.

U.S. Department of Health and Human Services. (1990). *Seventh special report to the U.S. Congress on alcoholism and health*. (DHHS Pub. No. (ADM)87-1519). Washington, D.C.: Superintendent of documents, U.S. Printing Office.

Young, T. J. (1988). Substance use and abuse among Native Americans. *Clinical Psychology Review*, *8*, 125-138.

Weibel-Orlando, J. (1987). Culture specific treatment modalities: Assessing client-to-treatment fit in Indian alcohol programs. In W. M. Cox (Ed.), *Treatment and prevention of alcohol problems. A resource manual* (pp. 261-283). Orlando, FL: Academic Press.

Westermeyer, J. (1987). Cultural patterns of drug and alcohol use: An analysis of host and agent in the cultural environment. *Bulletin on Narcotics*, *XXXIX*(2), 11-27.

Williams, G. D., Stinson, F. S., Parker, D. A., Harford, T. C., & Noble, J. (1987). Demographic trends, alcohol abuse and alcoholism. 1985-1995. *Alcohol Health and Research World*, *11*(3), 80-83.

Wright, J. D., Knight, J. W., Weber-Burdin, E., & Lam, J. (1987). Ailments and alcohol. Health status among the drinking homeless. *Alcohol Health and Research World*, *11*(3), 22-27.

Zeiner, A. R. (1980, October). *Biological sensitivity to alcohol*. Paper presented at the International Research Workshop, Long Beach, CA.

Appendix 1

APPENDIX 1

Diagnostic Screening Center Intake Log

DSC NUMBER	CLIENT NAME (PRINT)	RESIDENCE	CULTURE	AGE	SEX	ENTER DATE

DATE—————————————— PAGE——————

TIME	BAC	WAY	COND	CHEM	EXIT DATE	TIME	BAC	STATUS

APPENDIX 1 (continued)

DSC LOG CODES

Res. Status

1 = Homeless
2 = Staying with friends
3 = Staying with family
4 = From out of town (in Anch < 2 weeks)
5 = From out of state
6 = Rent (include hotel/motel)
7 = Other _____

Cultural Group

1 = Causian
2 = Black
3 = Am Indian
4 = Athabascan
5 = Tlingit
6 = Haida

Way Entered

1 = CSP
2 = APD
3 = ANS referral
4 = Walk in

5 = BFS referral
6 = Beans referral
7 = Cross Over House referral
8 = API referral
9 = Other (specify)

Cultural Group

7 = Yupik
8 = Inupiat
9 = Hispanic
10 = Asian
11 = Aleut
12 = Other _____

Status **(Where did they "go" when they left?)**

Refered To:
1 = BFS
2 = Beans
3 = ANS
4 = APD/Jail
5 = **Friends/Family Res.**
6 = **Own Res.**
7 = **Street**
8 = **Detox**
9 = **Other** _____
10 = **Humana**
11 = **API**
12 = **Providence**

Chemical

1 = Alcohol
2 = Drugs
3 = Alcohol & drugs

Condition Entered

1 = Unassisted normal walk
2 = Staggering
3 = Needed help walking
4 = Unconscious
5 = Don't know

Appendix 2

APPENDIX 2

Initial Screening Interview
Diagnostic Screening Center

Note

If any of the following conditions exist, seek medical attention immediately: Profuse bleeding - Severe pain - Difficulty breathing - Violent shakes, alcoholic seizures - Head injury in last 24 hours with dizziness, blurred vision, or difficulty walking.

DATE_____ DSC# _____ SACC#_____

Part I. Identifying Information

1. What is your name_____

2. What is your date of birth_____

3. ___Male ___Female

4. What is your social security Number?_____

5. What cultural group do you belong to?

___ Caucasian	___ Eskimo (__Yupik __ Inupiat)
___ Black	___ Hispanic
___ Am. Indian	___ Other AK Native_____
___ Athabascan	___ Asian
___ Tlingit	___ Aleut
___ Haida	___ Other_____

6. Are you:
 ___ Married (# years _____)
 ___ Living as married (How long? _____)
 ___ Separated (How long? _____)
 ___ Divorced (How long? _____)
 ___ Widowed (How long? _____)
 ___ Never married

7. Do you have any children?
  ___ No ___Yes (How Many?_____)

8. Are you a veteran? ___ No ___ Yes
 8a. Branch of service_____

 8b. Did you serve in Vietnam? ___ Yes ___ No

9. Did you finish high school? ___ Yes ___ No

 9a. What was the highest grade you completed?_____

10. What is your Spiritual belief?
   ___ Catholic   ___ Lutheran
   ___ Native American Church   ___ Baptist
   ___ Protestant   ___ Episcopal
   ___ Russian Orthodox   ___ Mormon
   ___ Congregational   ___ Methodist
   ___ None   ___ Other_____

11. Have you attended any church services in the past year?
   ___ No
   ___ Yes (How often did (do) you go?_____)

12. Are you working now?
   ___ Yes (Where?_____)
   ___ No (When was the last time you worked?_____)

13. What did you do on your last Job?_____

14. What kind of work do you usually do?_____

15. What do you consider to be your occupation? _____

Part 2. Living Arrangements

16. Do you have a regular place to stay?   ___ Yes **(Skip to # 22)**   ___ No **(Continue)**

17. Where do you usually sleep?

   ___ Street   ___ Camp-Out (Where_____)
   ___ BFS Shelter   ___ Relatives Residence
   ___ Friends Residence   ___ Other_____

18. Where did you spend last night?

   ___ Street   ___ Camp-Out (Where_____)
   ___ BFS Shelter   ___ Relatives Residence
   ___ Friends Residence   ___ Sleep -Off
   ___ Other_____

19. During the past few weeks, have you slept in . . . ? **(Circle one answer for each option below)**

	Yes	No	DK	NR
Your own house or apartment	1	2	7	8
A rooming house	1	2	7	8
A hotel or motel	1	2	7	8
A friend's place	1	2	7	8
A relative's place	1	2	7	8
A halfway house	1	2	7	8
In a jail or prison	1	2	7	8
A hospital or institution	1	2	7	8
Detox	1	2	7	8
The street	1	2	7	8
A car, truck or van	1	2	7	8

20. Of the places that were just mentioned, which do you say at most of the time?_____

APPENDIX 2 (continued)

21. How frequently do you stay on the street?   Would you say . . . . ?

> __Once a week
> __Two to three times a week
> __Every day
> __Don't know
> **Skip to Question 29**

22. Are you renting ___ or do you own ____ ....? **NO____ (Go to # 27)**

> ___ a room...... is this is a house____ apartment ____ hotel ____
> ___ an efficiency   apartment____ Condo ____
> ___ a one bedroom   apartment____ House _____ Condo ____
> ___ a two bedroom   apartment____ House _____ Condo ____
> ___ other _____

23. Do you stay there alone? __Yes __ No - With who do you stay with? _____

24. How long have you stayed there? _____

25. Did you stay there all of this week? ___Yes ___No (Where did you stay? _____)

26. Did you stay there all of last week? ___Yes ___No (Where did you stay? _____)

                                                               Go to #28

27. Do you stay with ....?

> ___ family _____ friends ____ other : _____

28. Do you consider this to be your permanent home?
> __Yes **(Go to Q# 29)**   __No **(Continue)**

> **28a.** Where do you consider your permanent home to be?_____)

29. Where did you live before? _____

30. How long did you stay there? _____

31. Did you stay there alone?
> ___ Yes
> ___No (Who do you stay with?_____)

Part 3. Drinking Behavior

32. When you drink, how much do you usually drink during a day's time?_____

33. What do you usually drink?_____

34. How much did you drink before you came here today?_____

35. How old were you when you started to drink regularly?_____

36. How long have you been on this binge?_____

37. Is there someone you usually drink with? __No __Yes - Who?_____

38. Have you ever thought about stopping? ___ Yes ___ No (Why? _____)

Part 4. Treatment History

39. Have you ever been in a detox facility before?   ___ No - **Go to Q.41** ___ Yes - **Continue**
    Where?......... (**Ask all below..**)
    ___ SACC - How many times? _____
    ___ Out of town
    (name town & detox facility) _____ # of times _____
    ___ Out of state
    (name state & detox facility) _____ # of times _____

40. When was the last time you were in detox?_____

41. Have you ever been in an alcohol treatment program? ___ No - **Go to Q.42** ___ Yes - **Continue**
    Where?......... (**Ask all below..**)
    ___ SACC - Which program? _____

    Did you finish the program? _____Yes _____No- Why? _____

    ___ ARP- Did you finish the program? _____Yes _____No - Why? _____

    ___ Nugens Ranch - Did you finish the program? _____Yes _____No - Why? _____

    ___ Out of town: (name town & treatment facility) _____

    Did you finish the program? _____Yes _____No - Why? _____

    ___ Out of state: (name state & treatment facility) _____

    Did you finish the program? _____Yes _____No - Why? _____

    ___ Other (in Anchorage) _____

    Did you finish the program? _____Yes _____No - Why? _____

Part 5. Family History

42. Are your mother and father still living?
    Mother ___Yes ___No
            (Alcohol related death? ___Yes ___No ___ Don't know)
    Father ___Yes ___ No
            (Alcohol related death? ___ Yes ___No ___ Don't know)

43. Did (do) your parents drink?
       ___ No
       ___ Yes (Who? ___ Father ___ Mother)

44. Does any anybody else in your family drink?
       ___ No
       ___ Yes (Who?_____)

45. Has anyone in your family ever had a drinking problem?
       ___ No
       ___ Yes (Who?_____)

APPENDIX 2 (continued)

Part 6. Other Drugs

46. Besides alcohol, have you ever used any other drugs?
    ___ No **(Go to Q.48)**
    ___ Yes
        Which? (Check all that apply)
            ___ Marijuana (Last use?_____)
            ___ Crack (Last use?_____)
            ___ Cocaine ("Snow" "Blow" "Coke")
                Last use?_____
            ___ Amphetamines ("Uppers" "Speed" "Crank" "Meth"
                "Crosstops" "Black Beauties")
                Last use?_____
            ___ Hallucinogens
                ___ LSD (Last use?_____)
                ___ Mushrooms (Last use?_____)
                ___ Angel Dust (Last use?_____)
            ___ Barbiturates ("Reds" "Yellows" "Ludes")
                Last use?_____
            ___ Heroin ("Smack") (Last use?_____)
            ___ Tranquilizers (Valium, Librium)
                Last use?_____
            ___ Inhalants (Gasoline, Butyl Nitrate, Amyl Nitrate)
                Last use?_____

47. Have you ever been in a drug treatment program?
    ___ No
    ___ Yes
        When?_____

        Where?_____

        How Long?_____

        Did you complete it? ___ Yes ___ No

48. Have you been in a hospital during the past month?
    ___ No
    ___ Yes
        What For?_____

Part 7. Legal Status

49. Have you ever been in jail?
    ___ No
    ___ Yes

50. Have you been in jail during the past year?
    How Long_____

    What for?_____

    Are you on probation? ___ No   ___ Yes

Appendix 3

APPENDIX 3

**Blood Alcohol Level and Behavioral Effects
Classification Categories[1]**

_____

Classification Category	Blood Alcohol Level	Behavioral Effect
Midly Intoxicated	.001-.055	Lowered efficiency of the cortex in the uppermost part of the brain. Lowered alertness, feeling good, beginning of release of inhibitions, start of impairment of judgment.
Intoxicated	.056-.155	At lower level, continued depression of the cortex, with reduced operation of those parts of the brain controlling movement, evolving, at higher level, to
Moderately Intoxicated	.156-.200	Progressive deterioration of higher Cortical functions and some motor activities. Slowed of reaction time and impairment of motor functioning, greater sense of release of inhibitions, noticeable clumsiness, talkativeness, impairment of peripheral vision. Decrease in reaction time and motor performance, staggering, slurred speech, blurred vision, loss of judg ment, impairment of intellectual functioning.
Highly Intoxicated	.201+	At lower level, decreased midbrain functioning. Marked Intoxication. Depression in sensory and motor functioning. At higher level (.300+), Reduced functioning of lower portion of the brain - marked by increasing diffi- culty to maintain motor functioning; in- tellectual and sensory functions greatly impaired. At higher levels depression of entire brain functioning. Behavior can range from being boisterous and belligerent to stupor and confusion, to unconsciousness. A BAL greater than .40 can lead to death.

_____

[1] Derived from Ray & Ksir (1990) and Segal (1988).